PERSONAL DEDICATION

NIPISSING - PARRY SOUND CATHOLIC DISTRICT SCHOOL BOARD

INSPIRING AND FUN
STORIES & PICTURES OF
THE HEROES OF OUR STUDENTS

**Barry Spilchuk
Gerald G. Amond**

You're My Hero Books Ltd.
Head Office - North Bay, Ontario
Executive Office – Toronto, Ontario Canada

www.YMHbooks.com

Library of Congress Cataloging-in-Publication Data

You're My Hero - Nipissing - Parry Sound Catholic District School Board. Inspiring and fun stories of the heroes of the students of our school system. / Barry Spilchuk, Gerald. G. Amond and the students of the Nipissing-Parry Sound Catholic District School Board.

ISBN 978-1-4276-3419-1 (trade paper)
1. Inspiration - I. Spilchuk, Barry; II Amond, Gerald G.; III Title; You're My Hero - Nipissing - Parry Sound Catholic District School Board

© 2008 Barry Spilchuk and Gerald G. Amond

All rights reserved. Printed in the United States of America. No part of this publication may be reproduced, stored in a retrieval system or transmitted in any form or by any means, electronic, mechanical, photocopying, recording or otherwise, without the written permission of the publisher.

Publisher: You're My Hero Books Ltd.
             ONE Palace Pier Court, Suite 1904
             Toronto, ON Canada M8V 3W9

Executive Editor - Karen Spilchuk
Senior Editor - Carolyn Samuel
Cover design and layout - Laura Little
Cover Photo of Barry Spilchuk - Ed Eng

DEDICATION

FROM THE CHILDREN

With love and joy we dedicate this work to all students - past, present and future,
of the Nipissing - Parry Sound Catholic District School Board.
We also wish to dedicate this book to
PACKSACK FOR SMILES,
ONE KIDS PLACE
and children everywhere.

FROM BARRY

To a dear lady who has showed me that God is ALWAYS there for me.
And She, Like God, is always there for me ~
No Matter What. I call her Mom.
Everyone else calls her Joyce Spilchuk.

To a man who has showed me that WORK that you love is one of the nicest blessings
that God can bestow on you ~ My Dad ~ Eugene Spilchuk.
Thank you for ALL your support Dad.

FROM GERALD

There are so many people who I could use this space
to say, "I LOVE YOU," to.
My wife, Teresa, you are my rock and my best friend.
My son, Matt, you have made me so proud - every moment of your life.
My mother, Julie. I love you so much.
Thank you - for EVERYTHING!

**We love our Heroes!
Who is YOUR Hero?**

MAY WE MAKE A SUGGESTION?

If you have taken the time to share your Hero's name with us, you should find both of your names on the Honour Roll that starts on the next page.

If you are giving this book to your Hero, you may want to take a moment and say something like,

"We have known each other for awhile. I honour you as a friend (or family member) and I wanted you to know - you are one of my heroes too."

If you are the Hero who has been named in this book, take a second and think about what has just happened.

Someone took the time to think about who their hero is. They even took the time to share it with us.

And they picked...You!

Authors and Heroes

HONOUR ROLL

Location: If a ***number*** *is shown, the story can be found on that specific page in this book. If the letters* ***WS*** *are shown, the story can be seen on our website: www.YMHbooks.com Please click on CURRENT PROJECTS and scroll down to CSB (Catholic School Board).*

Writer's Name	Hero's Name	Location
Aiton, Melanie	Wendy Aiton	70
Alcock, Trevor	Greg Grisé	WS
Allard, Julia	Simone Skuro	104
Amyotte, Vanessa	Mrs. Hegyi	8
Angelo, Allison	Lori Angelo	WS
Angelo, Allison	Grandpa	WS
Armstrong, Angel	Lucas Armstrong	WS
Armstrong, Lucas	Mrs. Cox	WS
Arnott, Alex	Wayne Gretzky	160
Assance-Goulais, Miigwans	Griffin Assance-Goulais	146
Assance-Goulais, Griffin	Hiram Monage	WS
Aubin, Courtney	Ivan & Rebecca Aubin	184
Audet, Amber	Tammy Desbois	WS
Audet, Cole	Mme. Levac	140
Aultman, Bobby	David Aultman	WS
B. B.	Mrs. D.	WS
Babak, Michelle	Marketa	WS
Baker, Alex	My Brother	138
Baker, Tyler James	Terry Fox	WS
Bakker-Orr, Jerrett	My Dad	219
Barrett, Sabrina	Andrea Cousineau	194

Writer's Name	Hero's Name	Location
Beaucage, Bianca	Police Officers	139
Beaucage, Blake	Nimosh the Dog	209
Beaucage, Devin	My Dad	141
Beaucage, Isadore	Milton Beaucage	WS
Beaucage, Julia	Paulette Beaucage	WS
Beaucage, Sabrina	Devin Beaucage	WS
Beaucage, Skyler	Katelynn Q.	WS
Beaucage, Syler	Gail Beaucage Commanda	218
Beaucage-Couchie, Maysin	Gail Beaucage Commanda	145
Beauchamp, Javen	My Grandma	WS
Beaulieu, Justine Emily	Aunt Alisha	WS
Becker, Kierra	Nurses	144
Belford, Brody	Jack Belford	WS
Bellaire, Lakin	Adwenna Peters	WS
Belong, Montana	Stacey Gingras	WS
Bénard-Legris, Ashley Rose	Rosa Parks	155
Bénard-Legris, Ashley Rose	My Parents & Grandparents	WS
Benoit, Brady	Aimee Osas	79
Berthiaume, Kyle	Dan Berthiaume	WS
Bessette, Broedy	Jake Piché	WS
Birmingham, Mason	John Thayer	128
Bitonti, Talia	Jessica Sheldon	WS
Blunt, Connor	My Dad	WS
Boden, Brock	Uncle Brock	WS
Boileau, Brady	Kurtiss David	28
Boissoneau, Allen Jr.	Allen Boissoneau	WS
Bolan, Emily	John Bolan	WS
Bolan, Stephanie	John Bolan	WS
Bonnah Miyah,	Lark and Les Bonnah	200
Boudreau, Jacob	Nick	WS
Boudreau Kellar, Owen	My Hero	WS
Bourssa, Pierre Jr.	John Campeau	WS
Bowhey, Amber Rose	Jaja	WS
Bowhey, Cole	Grandma	WS
Brazeau Sharp, Ericka	Mom and Dad	142

Writer's Name	Hero's Name	Location
Brazeau, Megan	Mom	WS
Brazeau, Taylor	Tracy Brazeau	WS
Breadmore, Sean	Maman Breadmore	WS
Breadmore, Tyler	Al Gore	WS
Breadmore, Tyler	Trooper the Dog	212
Brouillette, Alexandra	My Dog Shelby	WS
Brouillette, Kiara	Lise Bellaue	109
Brown, Courtney	The Kids in the LAC	5
Brownlee, Cristina	My Grandparents	WS
Brunet, Joshua	Paul Brunet	WS
Brunet, Matthew	Paul Brunet	WS
Buckley, Madison	Margaret Head	WS
Buckley, Robert	Dad	WS
Burden, Harley	Brad Burden	42
Burgess, Emma Lee	Sharon Larmand	112
Burnett, Tyler	Kyle Sheedy	WS
Butler, Breanna	Papa et Maman	WS
Byrko, John	Jason Beaucage	WS
C, Jessica	Loreen C.	WS
Caliciuri, Anthony	Al Gore	154
Caliciuri, Melissa	Gerhild Hildebrand	WS
Cangiano, Joe	Father Brian McKee	2
Cardelli, Angelina	Chantalle Cardelli	WS
Cardelli, Angelina	Shelby	WS
Cardelli, Dana	Chantalle Cardelli	72
Carter, Andrew	Sgt. Brunet	WS
Carter, Robert	Andrew Carter	WS
Castiglione, Kara	Vito Castiglione	52
Castiglione, Lia	Miss Clark	14
Cayen, Austin	Mom and Dad	138
Cerasia, Dayton	Danielle Cerasia	WS
Cerisano, Connor	Jon Cerisano	54
Cesarano, Ava	Jana Stezka	WS
Cesarano, Maya	Jesus Christ	WS
Chan, Sieara	Mickey Chan	WS

Writer's Name	Hero's Name	Location
Chayer, Matthew	Mike Chayer	216
Chenier, Emilly	John McGrinder	125
Chew, Kenisha	Michelle Chew	WS
Cicciarelli, Nicholas	Mark Cicciarelli	56
Clark, Mackenzie	Carolyn and Ron Clark	197
Class of Grade 3	Colleen Taylor	WS
Commanda, Brent	Brooklyn Thompson	WS
Commanda, Drake	Pam Commanda	141
Commanda, Jamie	Shadow Commanda	53
Commanda, Madison	Dad	WS
Coniconde, Jesta	Jesus Christ	WS
Contant, Meuriza	J P Contant	WS
Cook, Victoria	Grandpa	WS
Cormier, Kaitlyn	Fred Cormier	46
Costante, Brooke	Carly Levinski	WS
Costello, Kalyah	Doyle Costello	WS
Côté, Alanah Maureen	Cindy Belanger	178
Côté, Olivia	Alexiss Meecham	27
Cottreau-Bossert, Robert	Ma Grandmere	WS
Cottreau-Bossert, Robert	Mom	WS
Couch, Jenna	John Couch	WS
Couch, Jamey	Renata Couch	WS
Couchie, Mackenzie	Alyssa Couchie	WS
Couchie, Shandace	Grandma & Grandpa	147
Courchesne, Erica	Dad	WS
Crescenzi, Brianna	Jesus Christ	WS
Cucullo, Adam	Bob Lawryniw	130
Cushing, Nicholas	Uncle Rich	WS
D. Taylor	Zoey La Chienne	WS
Dagg, Emilie	Mom and Dad	141
Dagg, Ian	John Gilligan	WS
Dagg, Taylor	Kathy Dagg	WS
D'Agostino, Elaine	Stefano D'Agostino	126
Danis, Kyle	Sean Danis	144
Decaire, Brittany	Le Soldats	WS

Writer's Name	Hero's Name	Location
Decaire, Brittany	My Parents	WS
Decaire, Greg	Derek Decaire	176
Decaire, Nickolas	Daynen Murphy	WS
Decaire, Nickolas	Jerry	WS
Decost, Kyleigh	Dave Decost	122
Degagne, Kylie	Degagne Family	WS
Demers, Jesse	Gina Demers	WS
Demers, Karli	Gina & Greg Demers	WS
Derosier, Evan	Rob Desrosier	220
Derosier, Parker	Rob Desrosier	WS
Desbiens, Joshua	J.C. Desbiens	60
Desormeau, Taylor	My Parents	WS
Desormiers, Nickolas	Jeff Desormiers	WS
Desroches, Adam	Shawn Pichokie	WS
Desroches, Alexander	Tubby the Dog	WS
Desroches, Rebecca	Mom	WS
Desrosiers, Nadia	Josie Desrosiers	74
Dietrich, Chelsea	My Friends	29
DiLello, Aidan	Mark DiLello	50
Dobbs, Michael	Dad	WS
Dokis, Evan	Eddie Black	WS
Domander, Jacqueline	Andrea Parks	218
Doyle, Caela	My Grandma	WS
Driver, Matthew	Mom and Dad	WS
Dube, Jennifer	Bonnie McCann	143
Dubeau, Jacob	Dave Tralevan	88
Ducharme, Dylan	Elaine Ducharme	WS
Ducharme, Jerrod	Brenda Ducharme	217
Dufresne, Sara	North Bay Police	91
Duhaime, Fraser	Trevor Alcock	166
Dunn, Kassidy	Amanda Dunn	WS
Durocher, Kayleigh	Linda Teeple	105
Duchesne, Gabrielle	Shirley Duchesne	113
E. El.	My Hero	WS
Ethier, Ryan	My Hockey Coach	WS

HONOUR ROLL

Writer's Name	Hero's Name	Location
Eves, Robyn	Mother and Father	WS
F. MJ	Jay Fraser	WS
Falconi, Brianna	Jessie Falconi	WS
Falconi, Holly	Aunt Rose	WS
Farley, Kayla	Mitsy	WS
Farrell, Sierra	Auntie Diane	WS
Faubert, Tyler	Lisa Faubert	WS
Ferrigan, Coleman James	Kevin Ferrigan	218
Ferrigan, Riley	Spiderman	146
Filiatrault, Austen	Cole Filiatrault	WS
Fisher, Hayley Faith	Stacey Fisher	143
Fleury, Jo-anna	Mr. Jacques	11
Foisy, Serena	Claire Foisy	107
Fok, Nathan	Karen Fok	WS
Fong, Kyesha	Kim Munro	173
Fournier, Tony	Jesus Christ	222
Fryer, Hailee	Mon Pere	WS
Fuerth, Isabelle	Ryan Fuerth	55
Fulford, Corey	Joyce Daniels	7
G. Daniel	Marc R.	WS
Gaboury, Avery	Brutes Gaboury	208
Gale, Brittany Lauren Ashley	Jamie McQuaid	174
Gardiner, Braidyn-Lynn	Sherry Gardiner	WS
Gaudreau, Benjamin	Charlotte Gaudreau	WS
Gauthier, Mallory	Joan Gauthier	WS
Gauthier, Sarah	Patrick Petri	WS
George, Kiley	Uncle Cameron	144
George, Lillian	Meriza & Ervin George	WS
George, Mickey	Dudley George	WS
Gillespie, Whisper	Pennie Gillespie	WS
Gillespie, Meadow	Moonstar Gillespie	WS
Gilligan, John	Val & Carey Gilligan	WS
Gilligan, Mackenzie	Aline Gilligan	WS
Gilligan, Shannon Patricia	Aline Gilligan	WS
Gingras, Marc-Andre	Anne Gingras	WS

Writer's Name	Hero's Name	Location
Giroux, Simon	Ma Soeur	WS
Giroux, Tagen	Maman - Vandi Kennedy	217
Gorecki, Vicky	Katie Svenson	32
Goulais, Benjamin Dixon	Keith Goulais	WS
Goulais, Darian	Kyle Goulais	WS
Goulais, Hailey	Michael & Geraldine Goulais	142
Goulais, Morgan	God	WS
Goulais, Sylvain Fernand	Grandpa	WS
Goulais, Weston	Josh Goulais	WS
Goulais - McLeod, Richard	The Underdog	WS
Grade 3 Class	Coleen Taylor	4
Gravelle, Laureena	Grandpa	WS
Gregson, Mackenzie	Frances Lees	114
Gregson, Mackenzie	Ashley Tisdale	WS
Gregson, Spencer	Jesus Christ	WS
Grubé, Alyssa-Marie	Mom and Dad	WS
Guénette, Gracie	Philip Guénette	217
H. B.	My Dad	WS
H. D.	My Dog Chief	WS
Haggart, Tyler	Noah Haggart	WS
Harkness, Brandon	My Opa	WS
Harkness, Julia Anne	Kelsey Michaud	30
Harmon, Jessica	Scott Harmon	WS
Harrison, Han Kyuri	Terry Fox	WS
Hart, Savannah	Mlle Savard	WS
Harvey, Brandon	My Dad	WS
Harvey, Deanna	Chief The Dog	141
Hebert, Curtis	Shelley Dubeau	95
Heffern, Claudia	Rodney St. Denis	57
Heil, Emily	Lisa Heil	WS
Hodgson, Carter	Madeleine and Loren Chadbourn	188
Hokstad, Hans	Serena Foisy & Katie Hokstad	198
Hubert, Gabrielle	Rachel Robertson	WS
Hubley, Bradley	Jennifer Hubley	WS
Hummel, Taylor	Mark Hummel	40

Writer's Name	Hero's Name	Location
Hurley, Alexander	Dr. Carter	94
Hurley, Alexander	My Friends	WS
Hurtubise, Elliauna	Keitha Hurtubise	WS
Hutul, Sam	Grandpa - Bill Hutul	WS
Ibbitson, Josée	Traci Ibbitson	WS
Jackson, Sylvie	Sam Jackson	58
Jeanneault, Kyle	Dad	WS
Jedynak, Hailey	Skyler Beaucage	WS
Jennea, Kyle	Mon Pere	WS
Jodouin, Brandon	Ashley Jodouin	WS
Joiner, Owen	Mme Klein et Matthew	10
Jones, Taylor	Kyle Shewfelt	159
Justice, Amanda	Lucy Cox	WS
K. Amanda	Trudy Haffner	WS
Kansala, Cooper	Sean Kansala	WS
Kelly, Liam	Sidney Crosby	WS
Kelly, Sean	My Mom and Dad	WS
Kervin, Caitlyne	Grandmaman	WS
Kirik, Emma	Yvette Brisson	WS
Kirik, Olivia	Mes Animeaux	WS
Knight, Brody	Uncle Bert	169
Kramp, Kennedy	Jason Kramp	WS
Krieg, Kayla	Cecile Karius	WS
Kulikowski, Michael	Stanley Kulikowski	219
L. Emily	Daniel Westenenk	WS
L. P.	Dad	WS
L. Riley	My Hero	WS
L. T.	Rusty the Dog	WS
Labelle-Viens, Channelle	The Hero in All of Us	WS
Lacelle, Brooklynn	Mindy	WS
Lachance, Jaydon	Spiderman	143
Ladouceur, Brooklyn	Sarah McLaughlin	158
Lafleur, Michael	Patrick Lafleur	WS
Lafleur, Patrick	Dad	WS
Lafond, Hannah	Dianne Andrusiek	WS

Writer's Name	Hero's Name	Location
Laforge, Emily	Samantha West	**142**
Laforge, Sierra	Samantha West	WS
Lajambe, Dayton	Uncle Jay	WS
Lamabe, Jodi	Nancy White	WS
Lamothe, Conrad	Fern Leo Lamothe	WS
Lamothe, Dawn	Patricia Sutherland	**66**
Lamothe, Emily	Daniel Westenenk	WS
Lariviere, Cody	Wendy Lariviere	WS
Lariviere, Logan	Wendy Lariviere	**145**
Laronde, Vanessa	Shaelyn Laronde	**196**
Latour, Cassandra	Ambulance Attendant	WS
Latour, Dustin	Dad	WS
Latour, Jonathan	Mom and Dad	WS
Lavallee, Anita	Mom	WS
Lavergne, Bradley	Tammy Lavergne	WS
Lavergne, Cody	Moe Lavergne	WS
Lavergne, Kassidy	Tammy & Moe Lavergne	WS
Lavergne, Riley	Spiderman	**147**
Lavigne, Todd	My Dog Rusty	WS
Lavoie, Jessica	Paula Lavoie	WS
Lavoie, Paul	Cody	WS
Lavoie, Paul	Steve Lavoie	WS
Leach, P.J.	Pierre & Sherry Leach	WS
Leavens, Jeremy	Mom	**143**
Leblanc, Dominique	Dan Leblanc	WS
Leblond, Matthew	Jean-Marc Leblond	**43**
Leblond, Nicholas	Jean-Marc Leblond	WS
Leblond, Nick	Jean-Marc Leblond	WS
Lesage, Tatum	Rob Lesage	WS
Lesage, Tatum	Shadow	WS
Lesage, Tory	Marlene Buller & Robert Lesage	WS
Lewis, Farrah	Lisa Faubert	WS
Lodge Emma,	North Bay Fire Fighters	**86**
Lortie, Sydney-Rose	Denis Lortie	WS
Luxton, Abby	My Family & Pets	WS

Writer's Name	Hero's Name	Location
Lyle, Brody	Douglas Bailey	WS
Lynn, Chelsea	Tyler Martin	186
M. C.	Erika	WS
M. JA	Travis	WS
MacAulay, Glen	Mallory MacAulay	142
MacDonalad, Joshua	Helga & Heinz Weiskopf	190
MacDonell, Shannon	Kathy Gaudreau	WS
Macpherson, Rory	Terry Fox	157
Madore, Alexis	Harry Potter	WS
Makuch-Francoeur, Kindrie	April Gardiner	WS
Makuch-Francoeur, Leif	My Dad, Josh	WS
Males, Stacey	Colleen Hutson	WS
Malette, Brooke	Grandpa	139
Masson, Ethan	Papa Masson	WS
Mathias, Amber	Catherine Mathias-MacDonald	172
Mathias, Demi	Linda Mathias	110
Matte, Abigail	Christine Matte	WS
Matte, Alexandra	Grandma Matte	WS
Maurice, Cory	Howard Davis	WS
Maurice, Courtney	Brittany Ann James	WS
McArthur, Emma	Coach Brody	WS
McDonell, Kara	Mme Turgeon	WS
McDonell, Kara	Chris McDonell	48
McDonell, Taylor	Grandpa	WS
McKay, Katie	Ted McKay	WS
McLeod, Bella	John Campeau	171
McLeod, Gabriel	Chris Montgomery	WS
McLeod, Jaydan	Travis Lemieux	31
McLeod, Ravin	My Brother	146
McLeod, Tysin	Johnnie-Rennie Beaucage	WS
McLeod-Fisher, Summer	Candace Fisher	WS
McLeod-Penasse, Melcolm	Cameron McLeod	WS
McLeod-Shabogesic, Echo	Laurie McLeod-Shabogesic	WS
McParland, John	Antoinette McParland	WS
McParland, Maria	Antoinette McParland	WS

HONOUR ROLL

Writer's Name	Hero's Name	Location
McQuabbie, Marlanda	Carmaine McQuabbie	108
McWeeney, Keegan	Lisa & Phil McWeeney	WS
McWeeney, Shayla	Lisa McWeeney	WS
Meecham, Alexiss	Abby Rich	WS
Menard, Jesse	Jessie Menard	147
Mercer, Sierra	Arthur Mercer	WS
Michaud, Alia	Stephan Michaud	51
Michaud, Kelsey	Teena Cross	67
Michaud, Tyler	Stephan Michaud	WS
Michauville, Kaya	Tracy Michauville	77
Miller, Darren	Mom	WS
Mills, Alexiss	Mom	WS
Mills, Jayme	Diane Huart	WS
Miner, Dylan	Allen Fisher	WS
Minor, Jenna	Julia Minor	WS
Mogan, Cecilia	Greg Grisé	170
Molnar, Amanda	Steve Molnar	129
Moore, Bradon	Kevin Moore	WS
Moore, Kristen	Ross Reilly	WS
Morley, Kayla	Shirley Morley	WS
Morley, Tamara	Dad	WS
Morningstar, Anika	Julie-Ann Morningstar	WS
Morrison, Tyler	Marie Dolbeck	WS
Mullan, Connor	Uncle Bryan	177
Murphy, Daynen	Mickey Murphy	WS
Murphy, Samantha	Parents	WS
Murphy, Samantha	Sherry Walsh-Murphy	WS
Murphy, Taylor	Parents	WS
Murphy, Taylor	Remington Murphy	210
Myles, Christopher	Robyn Myles	140
Myles, Joshua	My Hero	144
N. Amy	Kayley	WS
Nadeau. Patrick	Dad	WS
Needs, Zachary	Terry Fox	WS
Neil, Alexandra	Madison	WS

Writer's Name	Hero's Name	Location
Neil, Cory	Katrina Neil	WS
Neil, Sierra	Antoinette McParland	90
Newman, Avery	Hershey - My Dog	211
Newman, Jackson	Leo Rainer	127
Niemela, Kayley	Amy Niemela	WS
NO LAST NAME - DANBY	DEBY SAMSON	WS
NO LAST NAME - E.L.E.	ROBYN - MY SISTER	WS
NO LAST NAME - EMMA	My Dad	WS
NO LAST NAME - JACK	My Cousin Brody	WS
NO LAST NAME - MARK	FOSTER PARENTS	WS
NO LAST NAME - MICHAEL	STANLEY	WS
NO LAST NAME - PATRICK	BONNIE	76
North, Hailee	Grand-Pere	WS
O. L.	Dad	WS
Olivier, Rebecca	Alfred Morin	131
Ollivier, Hailey	Shawna Ollivier	WS
Ollivier, Shawna	Hailey Ollivier	220
O'Shea, Liam	Bill O'Shea	WS
O'Shea, Lorena	Alexis Caruso	WS
Ouellette, Amy Brianne	God	138
Ouellette, Casey	Pam Ouellette	173
Ouellette, Tianna	Grandma	WS
P. C.	Mom	WS
P. P.	Bonnie Brewer	WS
Paquet, Nicole	Mme Dione Turgeon	13
Paul, Delana	Jayden Paul	WS
Paulin, Danielle	Grandpa	WS
Penasse, Brady	Raymond Penasse	WS
Penasse, Brock	Cherie Penasse	139
Penasse, Dakota	Mats Sundin	WS
Penasse, Hanna	Alice Fraser	WS
Penasse, Shawnee	Marian Poirier	168
Penasse-Adams, Brogan	Brooklyn Penasse	WS
Penasse-McLeod, Chase	Mom and Dad	140
Peplinskie, Jennilee	Murray Peavoy	6

Writer's Name	Hero's Name	Location
Perkins, Bradley	My Dog	WS
Peters, Adwena	Dane Peters	WS
Peterson-Galema, Ethan	Chris Galema	WS
Peterson-Galema, Matthew	Chris Galema	44
Petrie, Emily	Uncle Bill	WS
Pettella, Daniela	Caitlin Howard	35
Pettella, Michael	Vic Pettella	132
Philion, Darrien Richard	Dad	140
Philion, Jason T.	Shirley Philion	WS
Piché, Nicholas	Aunt Shirley	92
Piché, Riley	North Bay Fire Fighters	WS
Pitre, Joseph	Art Armstrong	WS
Poisson, Cody	My Opa	WS
Power, Michael-Anthony	Rino the Dog	214
Quesnel, Kaitlyn	Skyler S.	WS
Quesnel, Kayla	Tracy Quesnel	WS
Quinn, Kiera	Nana	WS
R. B.	Dale Earnhardt	WS
R. K.	Alison Raffaele	WS
R. Steven	Mon Grand Papa	WS
Raffaele, Kayla	Alison Raffeale	WS
Ragnitz, Alexander	Renee Ragnitz	WS
Rainville, Tyler	Joel Rainville	WS
Ray, Wylden	Vita Young	106
Redner, Destiny	Kiara Rees	WS
Remillard, Ian	Kobe Bryant	WS
Remillard, Tarah-Lynn	Guylain Mayotte	WS
Restoule, Sheldon	Ethan	WS
Ricciuto, Victoria	Michelle Ricciuto	68
Rice, Megan	Megan Chason	WS
Roach, Julia	Ema Monderie	WS
Roberge, Meagan	Kayla Q.	WS
Robinson, Jeremy	Mark Robinson	WS
Roffey, Melissa	Steven Roffey	WS
Rogers, Christopher	My Mom the Nurse	WS

Writer's Name	Hero's Name	Location
Rogers, Jacob	Dale Earnhardt Jr.	156
Rogers, Scott	Mom	WS
Rothwell, Abigail	Mom and Dad	WS
Roy, Riley	Robert Roy	WS
Russell, Alexus	Tanya Guillemette	WS
San Cartier, Damion	God	WS
Sands, Drew	Ray Sands Jr.	WS
Sands, Sissy	Ray Sands	WS
Schaefer, Selena	Dr. Pokrant	89
Schiavo, Mackenna	Stephanie Schiavo	WS
Schierl, Mason	Keri Schierl	80
Schierl, Morgan	Ma Soeur	WS
Schlueting, Pacey	Lori Schlueting	WS
Schmidt, Stephanie	My Friend	24
Sciuk, Selena	Julien Sciuk	WS
Scott, Judy	Tina Scott	WS
Shaw, Cathy	Dione Turgeon	12
Shaw, Cathy	God	WS
Shaw, Janet	Dieu	WS
Shaw, Janet	Jesus Christ	WS
Shaw, Janet	Our Neighbours	93
Sheedy, Kyle	Tyler Burnett	WS
Sheedy, Madison	Meredith & Andrew Sheedy	WS
Sherry, Steven	Bob Pincivero	121
Smart, Cassandra	Carrie Smart	WS
Smart, Emma	Carrie Smart	WS
Smart, Hayden	Carrie Smart	WS
Smart, Madyssen	Mom and Dad	WS
Smart, Owen	Carrie & Doug Smart	146
Smiley, Ryan	Darryl Adams	WS
Smith, Raven	Tammy Graham	WS
Smith, Sarina	Bryan Smith	WS
Solomom, Tia	Daphne	147
Sommerville, Danielle	Micheline Lamarche	WS
Sorenson - Trudeau, Amaya	My Mommy	138

Writer's Name	Hero's Name	Location
St. Denis, Aimee	Rod St. Denis	WS
St. Louis, Alex	Alexander Ovechkin	WS
St. Louis, Patrick	Ken Downton	34
St. Pierre, Brianna	Ma Tante	WS
St. Pierre, Brandon	Lianne St.Pierre	WS
St. Pierre, Cassandra	Aunt Tonja	WS
Stanton, Skylar	Lorraine	WS
Steeves, Kaitlyn	Grandma	WS
Stencill, Marcus	Les Pompiers	WS
Stewart, Grace	Lily Stewart	WS
Stickle, Megan	Alyssa Thibault	26
Stitt, Britanny	Abby Krajc	WS
Stone, Corey	Tracy Godon	71
Summers, Cedric	My Uncle Brent	216
Summers, Isabelle	Kurtis Summers	49
Sutherland, Natalie	Brent Sutherland	WS
Swackhamer, Samantha	Crystal Swackhamer	189
T. CL	Ray Comeau	WS
T. J.	Mom	WS
T-S. A.	Mom	WS
Taché, Jasmine	Keri Taché	WS
Thompson, Brooklyn	Trisha Jones	139
Tourigny, Ashley	Tina Tourigny	WS
Tourigny, Tina	Norm Tourigny	WS
Trecartin, Ethan	My Grandma	220
Tripp, Jennifer	Katie Tripp	WS
Tripp, Katherine	Rick Tripp	WS
Turner, McKayla	Maman et Papa	WS
Udeschini, Max	Diego Udeschini	124
Valentine, Emma	Bonnie Valentine	WS
Vanderlee, Emma	Rick Vanderlee	WS
Vanderlee, Keats	Keats Williamson	120
VanHorn, Katlyn	Troy VanHorn	WS
Venditli, Ryan	Ambulance Attendants	98
Villeneuve, Jasper	Mike Villeneuve	WS

Writer's Name	Hero's Name	Location
Virtanen-Murphy, Chelsea	Chris Murphy	WS
Vossen, Bobby	Dieu	WS
Vossen, Jessie	Maidie Vossen	216
Voyer, Alexis	Mom and Dad	WS
Voyer, Austin	Jody Voyer	WS
W. A.	Jennifer Sanche	WS
Walker, Kyle	Dad	WS
Waltenbury, Nicholas	Emergency Medical Services (EMS)	96
Waltenbury, Spencer	Allison Walsh	WS
Watson, Katlin	Sandra Lawrence	219
Watt, Logan	John Gilligan	145
Watt, Skylar	Jason Aubertain	WS
Welch, Alisabeth	Laurie Welch	WS
Welch, Ross	Sidney Crosby	161
White, Amanda	Gina Cicciarelli	115
White, Benjamin	My Mom and Dad	WS
White, Victoria	Winston the Dog	206
Whitnell, Ayden	Jennifer Sanche	WS
Wilson, Brady	Dad	WS
Winterburn, Madison	Rosie Winterburn	78
Winterburn, Stephanie	My Family	WS
Wolfe, Micaela	Ron Ott	WS
Zaba, Becky	Aunt Matty	WS
Zaba, Melissa	Dad	145

Greetings from
Anthony Rota
M.P. Nipissing-Timiskaming

Everyday heroes are the unsung champions of everyday acts of goodness. Heroes are often identified as strong, intelligent and daring. In reality it is the traits of courage, honesty, bravery and selflessness that are the overlooked qualities.

A hero can be somebody admired for outstanding character or achievements and often you are introduced to these people in the early years of education.

It could be a teacher who has inspired you to learn, or a friend or family member that has gone that extra mile. Whoever it is, the impact made on your life is something that will never be forgotten.

One thing is certain, the world is a better place because of the actions of heroes.

Congratulations to the Nipissing-Parry Sound Catholic District School Board on providing this opportunity for everyone to recognize those that are truly making a difference. I would also like to commend the contributors to this book for sharing your personal heroes with us and reminding us who the true heroes really are.

Sincerely,

signature

Anthony Rota MP

Greetings from
Monique Smith
M.P.P. Nipissing

Just what makes someone a hero? Over the span of a lifetime, the idea of a hero is bound to evolve. For a young child, a hero may be someone who scares away the monsters under your bed. Later in life, a hero might be a mom or dad, a teacher, a hockey coach, a youth group leader, or a police officer. Ultimately heroism is about giving of yourself for other people and the world around us.

I have had many heroes in my life; my mom and dad, who have shown such grace, love and compassion during difficult times in their lives while never veering from their commitment to their family and their community; people I have known who have faced serious medical issues and fought their battles with incredible courage and dignity; and, local volunteers who through their commitment to their local causes have improved the lives of many and our community as a whole.

Heroes like the ones highlighted in this book are vital to the make up of our community and are one of the biggest reasons that Nipissing is such a great place to live. As Canadians, we often suffer from a modesty that makes us reluctant to celebrate those around us as heroes. There are so many individuals in our communities whose generosity is truly heroic. I am thrilled that this book will allow some to be recognized and celebrated.

My staff and I would like to congratulate Barry Spilchuk and Penny Tremblay for raising over $27,000.00 for local charities with the first You're My Hero™ book.

I would like to thank Barry Spilchuk, Gerald Amond and all those who submitted stories for making this book possible and allowing us to celebrate North Bay as the great place it is and its citizens as the heroes they are.

Sincerely

Monique Smith

Greetings from
Glenn Cundari
North Bay & District Chamber of Commerce

On behalf of the North Bay & District Chamber of Commerce, I congratulate the Nipissing-Parry Sound Catholic District School Board and their students on their involvement in the second edition of the You're my Hero™ book.

I'm personally proud of our Chamber's involvement with Barry Spilchuk, a Past President of our organization and well-respected community member. It was so inspiring to see the abundance of wonderful stories in the first book, You're my Hero™ - North Bay.

Each of us has heroes that have shaped our lives, sometimes they are famous people but very often they are the people who closest to us. What a great way to say, "You're my Hero"!

To Barry, coauthor Gerald Amond and all the school children that participated by sharing who their heroes are - We wish you all the best on this project and we look forward to the joy these stories will bring to our communities.

Sincerely,

NORTH BAY AND DISTRICT
CHAMBER OF COMMERCE

Greetings from
Joanne Savage
Maire/Mayor
Municipality of West Nipissing

Il me fait plaisir à titre du conseil de rendre hommage à nos jeunes écrivains de Nipissing-Ouest et quel privilège!

Félicitation à nos jeunes écrivains : les élèves de l'Ecole "Our Lady of Sorrows" pour avoir participé à ce projet et d'avoir composé des passages imprimés dans ce livre. La lecture de ce livre apportera beaucoup de bonheur et de sourires. Vos passages et vos compositions contribueront envers ce succès.

It's a privilege on behalf of council to recognize and congratulate the students of the Lady of Sorrows School for their stories published in this special book. This special book will no doubt bring a lot of joy and smiles to its readers. Your stories will have contributed towards this success.

Again congratulation and looking forward to happy reading,

Joanne Savage
Maire/Mayor
Municipality of West Nipissing

Greetings from
Hector D. Lavigne
Mayor
Municipality of Callander

Il me fait plaisir à titre du conseil de rendre hommage à vous, les jeunes écrivains de Callander.

A big congratulations from Council and the Community of Callander on the launch of this great project.

We are very proud of our new Ste Therese School and all the students that attend. I am looking forward to the release of this " You're my Hero Book" and the stories you will tell.

In addition to the many copies that will be purchased by your families, friends and neighbors, it is only appropriate that we keep a copy of the book in our very own Callander Library so that we can share your stories over and over again and for generations to come!

Go Ste Therese Go!

Hector D. Lavigne,
Mayor
Municipality of Callander

Greetings from
Dean Backer
Mayor
Town of Mattawa

On behalf of the Town of Mattawa Municipal Council it gives me great pleasure to congratulate the students of St. Victor Separate School on their recent literary project which contributed to the success of "You're my Hero" publication.

Mayor Dean Backer
Town of Mattawa

Greetings from
Vic Fedeli
Mayor
City of North Bay

A hero is defined as a person who wins recognition by noble deeds. In my capacity as Mayor of the City of North Bay, I see real heroes everyday.

Most heroes are people whose noble deeds go unheralded, but certainly not unnoticed. They are the folks who give of themselves for the benefit of others.

They are the people who volunteer their time to help out at a seniors' home, or coach a little league team. They are the people who raise money to fight disease, or help a struggling family. They are the people who really look around themselves and identify the needs of other people, and then do what they can to help. They are the people who take a moment to brighten someone else's day.

These are the unsung heroes that make such a vital difference in the lives of everyone in our city. On behalf of the citizens of North Bay, I want to thank Barry, Gerald and all the contributors for shedding a little bit of light on these unheralded noble deeds and reminding us all who the real heroes in life truly are.

Victor Fedeli

DID YOU KNOW?

When Barry Spilchuk was working with the Chicken Soup for the Soul® team, they donated TWENTY-FIVE CENTS of almost every book sold to charity.

You're My Hero has learned from Chicken Soup's generosity and has decided to share the profits from each book with local charities.

You're My Hero is donating at least $8.00 of every book sold to local charities!

The Student's and School Board have decided to share the profits from this book with:

ONE KIDS PLACE
PACKSACK for SMILES

The way we can do that is because of the outstanding support from our Sponsors and Advertisers.

We respectfully request you take the time to read their ads as you see them placed at the end of some chapters… and…next time you are in their place of business – stop in and say, **"Thank you for supporting the children and their dreams!"**

ACKNOWLEDGEMENTS
By co-author - Barry Spilchuk

Dear God:

Thank You so much for giving the world, Your son, Jesus Christ. Thank You so much for allowing Him to sacrifice His life to wash away our sins.

Thank You for allowing Your Holy Spirit to live inside of us to power our hopes, our dreams and our service.

Thank You for giving us a new day, every day so we can start over to serve You in the highest and best possible way - by celebrating each other -Your children.

AMEN

We would also like to thank:

Our student story contributors - for without them there would obviously be no book... and a little less joy in the world.

The Teachers, Principals, Educational Assistants, Administrative staff, Secretarial staff and Custodial staff of each school, the Board, the Board staff, the Trustees and the Parents: THANK YOU for LOVING the children so much and being a beacon for the future. It really does "take a village" doesn't it?

ACKNOWLEDGEMENTS

Our sponsors and advertisers - it is their generosity and caring that has allowed us to sell books in a NEW WAY as we donate a minimum of $8.00 of each book sold to charity and celebrate our Heroes at the same time.

Our first book, YOU'RE MY HERO™ - NORTH BAY had the distinction of donating over $27,000.00 to local charities for two main reasons, the above mentioned sponsors and advertisers and the book-buying public of North Bay and area. They all welcomed the book with open arms and happy hearts. We are still hearing stories of how the first book touched so many people with its heartfelt stories and simple way of saying, "I love you."

Our sincere appreciation goes to Joanne Bénard, the Superintendent of the School Board. Joanne and her team immediately embraced the concept of how their students could celebrate their creativity and caring by writing stories from their hearts about their personal heroes.

I immediately knew this book would be wonderful when I sat in Joanne's office and we were chatting about school, children and Catholic Education. Joanne shared with me a story about one of her friends who asked Joanne the question, "Is it difficult working within the Catholic school system?" Joanne did not even hesitate with the answer. As I remember it, Joanne said, "I get to go to work everyday and be myself."

Our appreciation goes to Maryanne Neeley for her "whatever-it-takes" attitude to help get all the last minute things done.

Our thanks also goes to all the schools within the system, especially Our Lady of Sorrows in Sturgeon Falls and St. Alexander who had us in to speak with the students and teachers to share our vision and have some SILLY TIME with the children.

Our internal and "SILENT" support team deserves "kudos" for their never ending support and cheerleading: Karen, Michael, Chrissy, Jamie, Tim, Joyce and Eugene Spilchuk; Paul Barton and Marion Cook; David and Marcia Treat; Kenny Markanich and Brad Currie; Maria Speth, Randy Thomson, Joe and Ken Sinclair; Andy, Mary-Rose and Heather Little.

Our M.P. ~ Anthony Rota, Our MPP ~ Monique Smith, Our Chamber President ~ Glenn Cundari, Sturgeon Falls Mayor ~ Joanne Savage, Callander Mayor ~ Hec Lavigne, Mattawa Mayor ~ Dean Backer, North Bay Mayor ~ Vic Fedeli, Powassan Mayor ~ Bob Young for caring enough about our students that they took the time to share their words of support and encouragement for our young authors.

I would like to personally thank Suzanne Harmony for her big heart and intuitive spirit. Suzanne offered to be the coauthor of this book. The night we signed the contract, I shared with her and her partner, the amazing Dr. Mario Lemay, the fact that I was going to ask a friend of mine, Gerry Amond to coauthor the book until Suzanne offered her help. Suzanne knows Gerry and she knew about Gerry's health situation. The next day, Suzanne called me back and asked if was okay to withdraw from the project. "I feel in my heart that this book is Gerry's to do."

She was right. Merci beaucoup Suzanne, vous êtes incroyables!

To my coauthor, Gerry Amond, I love you brother.

You are a shining example of what it's like to be... a man. You are a wonderful father, devoted husband, admiring son, big-hearted brother, grateful Catholic, generous businessman and dear, dear friend to all who have the pleasure of seeing your smile, hearing your laugh and feeling your presence. Thank you for celebrating the children of the Nipissing-Parry Sound Catholic District School Board with me. It is my deep honour to share these pages with you.

Teresa and Matt Amond, I know you think that you are doing what any family would do given the circumstances that you are faced with. As Gerry is living with and healing from cancer, YES, you are doing all the things that any family would do. You are also stretching your imagination and celebrating life with Gerry to the highest and best of your abilities. Thank you for showing all of us what it is like to live life to the fullest - no matter what the circumstances.

A HUGE thank you to Cam Graham of JUST SPORTS by Cam. Your intuition and business savvy helped us in a special way.

Our deepest appreciation goes to Carolyn Samuel, the senior editor for this book (and the first book). Carolyn loves children and the celebration of their talents. She dove right in and loved this book from the beginning.

Félicitations à Mme Ginette Hamelin et Mlle Carolyn Samuel pour les révisions et corrections des textes en français. Toute l'équipe de YOU'RE MY HERO et les étudiants, disent, "MERCI BEAUCOUP" pour votre service.

Laura Little, you are amazing. Laura is the graphic and layout artist who made these pages come alive. Laura genuinely cares how each story and advertisement comes out. She wants each child and sponsor to know that their contribution is valued and appreciated.

Joyce Spilchuk, (Mom) thank you so much for welcoming me home and opening your home to me as we did our final two week editing and ad blitz. Your help in building our book is much appreciated.

Karen Spilchuk, my Executive editor, co-parent of our three children and forever friend, thank you for all your support and love through out the years. Thank you for caring for each story as if our own children wrote it. Your kindness and compassion shows in each story.

PUBLISHER'S NOTE:

I am always asking God for guidance and to show me if I am on the right track.

As I was finishing off "Hero Day" at Our Lady of Sorrows in Sturgeon Falls, I asked the children if they had any questions. One young girl stood up and said, *"How did you get such a good idea to do these Hero books?"*

I was so touched by such an insightful question from such a young girl I gave her a free book. I explained to her that I was working on another dream a few years ago and I prayed that God would help me find a way to help and honour people in cities all across Canada and the USA.

I shared with her that one day I got a call from a gentleman who told me about two, grade-six twin girls in Flint, Michigan that asked, *"Can we do a Chicken Soup book in our classroom?"* After some discussion, we determined that we were not able to do a Chicken Soup book in their classroom – BUT – we could do a book for the whole community. After two years of hard work, testing and planning we had come up YOU'RE MY HERO™.

The young girl at Our Lady of Sorrows immediately stood up and said that she had to tell me something really important. I joked that she probably just wanted another free book. What she said actually brought goose bumps to my arms and tears to my eyes and as I remembered my prayer about asking God if I was on the right track.

"Barry, I just wanted you to know, I am in grade-six AND I have a twin sister!"

Thank You God for answering my prayer. Again.

Barry

SPECIAL HERO DEDICATION

To a dear man who has showed us all how to love God and love others unconditionally:

Mr. Mike McCormick

Until his passing in 2008, he was a true friend to everyone, an incredible husband, a fantastic father and family man and a caring, loving Catholic.

When he passed, the Pepsi plant where he worked, closed down and rented a bus to take the employees to Mike's funeral to celebrate his life.

Mike – You are loved!

Barry

REWARD!!!
WANTED - YOUR EAGLE EYES

Be on the lookout for: spelling mistakes, typos, incorrect page numbers, improper grammar, oversights, and missed names.

Despite the heroic efforts of our team, we realize that we may have made a mistake or two along the way. We would love your help and input. If you find an error, please e-mail us.

As a **REWARD** for your help we will send
you an e-copy of our article entitled:

THE 12 KEYS TO PROSPERITY

Please send an e-mail and tell us what the error is and what page it is on: **oops@ymhbooks.com**

Thank you for being part of the You're My Hero™ team!

TABLE OF CONTENTS

Honour Roll vii
Community Greetings xxiii
Acknowledgments xxxii
Introduction xlvii
Director's Message xlix

CHAPTER ONE: OUR FAITHFUL HERO
    Father Brian McKee 2

CHAPTER TWO: HEROES IN OUR SCHOOLS
Collen Taylor by Grade 3 Class 4
The Kids in the LAC by Courtney Brown 5
Murray Peavoy by Jenilee Peplinskie 6
Joyce Daniels by Corey Fulford 7
Mrs. Hegyi by Vanessa Amyotte. 8
Mme Klein et Matthew by Owen Joiner 10
Mr. Jacques by Jo-anna Fleury 11
Dione Turgeon by Cathy Shaw 12
Madame Turgeon by N. Paquet 13
Miss Clark by Lia Castiglione 14

CHAPTER THREE: OUR FRIENDS

An Unlikely Friend by Stephanie Schmidt 24
Alyssa Thibeault by Megan Stickle 26
Alexis Meecham by Olivia Côté 27
Kurtis David by Brady Boileau 28
My Friends by Chelsea Dietrich 29
Kelsey Michaud by Julia Anne Harkness 30
Travis Lemieux by Jayden McLeod 31
Katie Svenson by Vicky Gorecki 32
Ken Downton by Patrick St. Louis 34
Caitlin Howard by Daniela Pettella 35

CHAPTER FOUR: OUR DADS

Mark Hummel by Taylor Hummel 40
Brad Burden by Harley Burden 42
Jean-Marc Leblond by Matthew Leblond 43
Chris Galema by Matthew Peterson - Galema 44
Fred Cormier by Kaitlyn Cormier 46
Chris McDonell by Kara McDonell 48
Kurtis Summers by Isabelle Summers 49
Mark DiLello by Aiden DiLello 50
Stephan Michaud by Alla Michaud 51
Vito Castiglione by Kara Castiglione 52
Shadow Commanda by Jamie Commanda 53
Jon Cerisano by Connor Cerisano 54
Ryan Fuerth by Isabelle Fuerth 55
Mark Cicciarelli by Nicholas Cicciarelli 56
Rodney St. Denis by Claudia Hefern 57
Sam Jackson by Sylvie Jackson 58
J.C. Desbiens by Joshua Desbiens 60

CHAPTER FIVE: OUR MOMS

Patricia Sutherland by Dawn Lamothe 66
Teena Cross by Kelsey Michaud 67
Michelle Ricciuto by Victoria Ricciuto 68
Wendy Aiton by Melanie Aiton 70
Tracy Godon by Corey Stone 71
Chantalle Cardelli by Angelina Cardelli 72
Pam Ouellette by Casey Ouellette 73
Josie Desrosiers by Nadia Desrosiers 74
Bonnie by Patrick 76
Tracy Michauville by Kaya Michauville 77
Rosie Winterburn by Madison Winterburn 78
Aimee Osas by Brady Benoit 79
Keri Schierl by Mason Schierl 80

CHAPTER SIX: OUR COMMUNITY

North Bay Fire Fighters by Emma Lodge 86
Dave Tralevan by Jacob Dubeau 88
Dr. Pokrant by Selena Schaefer 89
Antoinette McParland by Sierra Neil 90
North Bay Police Officers by Sara Dufresne 91
North Bay Fire Fighters by Riley Piché 92
Our Neighbours by Janet Shaw 93
Dr. Carter par Alexander Hurley 94
Shelley Dubeau by Curtis Hebert 95
Emergency Medical Services by Nicholas Waltenbury 96
The Ambulance Attendant by Ryan Venditli 98

CHAPTER SEVEN: OUR GRANDMOTHERS

Simone Skuro by Julia Allard 104
Linda Teeple by Kayleigh Durocher 105
Vita Young by Wylden Ray 106
Claire Foisy by Serena Foisy 107
Carmaine McQuabbie by Marlanda McQuabbie 108
Lise Bellaue by Kiara Brouillette 109
Linda Mathias by Demi Mathias 110
Sharon Larmand by Emma Lee Burgess 112
Shirley Duchesne by Gabrielle Duchesne 113
Frances Lees by Mackenzie Gregson 114
Gina Cicciarelli by Amanda White 115

CHAPTER EIGHT: OUR GRANDFATHERS

Keats Williamson by Keats Vanderlee 120
Bob Pincivero by Steven Sherry 121
Dave Decost by Kyleigh Decost 122
Diego Udeschini by Max Udeschini 124
John McGrinder by Emilly Chenier 125
Stefano D'Agostino by Elaine D'Agastino 126
Leo Rainer by Jackson Newman 127
John Thayer by Mason Birmingham 128
Steve Molnar by Amanda Molnar 129
Bob Lawryniw by Adam Cucullo 130
Alfred Morin, a Brave Heart by Rebecca Olivier 131
Vic Pettella by Michael Pettella 132

CHAPTER NINE: OUR HEROES IN PICTURES

My Brother by Alex Baker 138
God by Amy Ouellette 138

MaryAnn Trudeau by Amaya Sorensen Trudeau 138
Mom and Dad by Austin Cayen 138
Police Officers by Bianca Beaucage 139
Cherie Penasse by Brock Penasse 139
My Grandpa by Brooke Malette 139
Mommy by Brooklyn Thompson 139
Mom and Dad by Chase Penasse-McLeod 140
Mommy by Christopher Myles 140
Mme. Levac by Cole Audet 140
My Dad by Darrien Philion 140
My Dog Chief by Deanna Harvey 141
My Dad by Devin Beaucage 141
Pam Commanda by Drake Commanda 141
My Mom and Dad by Emilie Dagg 141
My Mom Samantha by Emily Laforge 142
Mom and Dad by Ericka Brazeau 142
Mallory MacAulay by Blen MacAulay 142
Michael & Geraldine by Hailey Goulais 142
Stacey Fisher by Hayley Faith Fisher 143
Spiderman by Jaydon Lachance 143
My Mom Bonnie McCann by Jennifer Dube 143
Mom & Dad by Jeremy Leavens 143
My Hero by Joshua Myles 144
Nurses by Kierra Becker 144
Uncle Cameron by Kiley George 144
Sean Danis by Kyle Danis 144
My Mom Wendy by Logan Lariviere 145
John Gilligan by Logan Watt 145
My Mommy Gail by Maysin Beaucage-Couchie 145

My Dad by Melissa Zaba 145
Griffin Assance-Goulais by Miigwans Assance-Goulais 146
Carrie & Doug Smart by Owen Smart 146
My Brother by Ravin McLeod 146
Spiderman by Riley Ferrigan 146
Spiderman by Riley Lavergne 147
Grandma & Grandpa by Shandace Couchie 147
Daphne by Tia Solomon 147
Jesse Menard by Jesse Menard 147

CHAPTER TEN: OUR CELEBRATED HEROES
Al Gore by Anthony Caliciuri 154
Rosa Parks by Ashley-Rose Bénard Legris 155
Dale Earnhardt Jr. by Jacob Rogers 156
Terry Fox by Rory Macpherson 157
Sarah McLaughlin by Brooklyn Ladoucer 158
Kyle Shewfelt by Taylor Jones 159
Wayne Gretzky by Alex Arnott 160
Sidney Crosby by Ross Welch 161

CHAPTER ELEVEN: OUR AUNTS & UNCLES
Trevor Alcock by Frasier Duhaime 166
Marian Poirier by Shawnee Penasse 168
Uncle Bert by Broday Knight 169
Greg Grisé by Cecelia Morgan 170
John Campeau by Bella Mcleod 171
Catherine Mathias-MacDonald by Amber Mathias 172
Kim Munro by Kyesha Fong 173
Jamie McQuaid by Brittany Lauren Ashley Gale 174

Derek Decaire by Greg Decaire 176
Bryan Mullan by Connor Mullan 177
Cindy Belanger Alanah Maureen Côté 178

CHAPTER TWELVE: OUR FAMILIES
Ivan and Rebecca Aubin by Courtney Aubin 184
Tyler Martin by Chelsea Lynn 186
Madeleine and Loren Chadbourn par Carter Hodgson 188
Crystal Swackhamer by Samantha Swackhamer 189
Helga and Heinz Weiskopf by Joshua MacDonald 190
Marketa by Michelle Babak 192
Brooklyn Thompson by Brent Commanda 194
Andrea Cousineau by Sabrina Barrett 195
Shaelyn Laronde by Vanessa Laronde 196
Carolyn and Ron Clark by Mackenzie Clark 197
Serena Foisy and Katie Hokstad by Hans Hokstad 198
Lark and Leslie Bonnah by Miyah Bonnah 200

CHAPTER THIRTEEN: OUR PETS
Winston by Victoria White 206
My Dog Brutes by Avery Gaboury 208
Nimosh the Dog by Blake Beaucage 209
Remington Murphy by Taylor Murphy 210
My Dog Hershey by Avery Newman 211
Trooper the Dog by Tyler Breadmore 212
Rino the Dog by Michael Anthony Power 214

CHAPTER FIFTEEN: HERO HIGHLIGHTS

Mike Chayer by Matthew Chayer 216
Maidie Vossen by Jessie Vossen 216
Uncle Brent Summers by Cedric Summers 216
Brenda Ducharme by Jerrod Ducharme 217
Vandi Kennedy by Tagen Giroux 217
Philp Guenette by Gracie Guenette 217
Andrea Parks by Jacqueline Domander 218
Gail Beaucage Commande by Syler Beaucage 218
Kevin Ferrigan by Coleman James Ferrigan 218
Sandra Lawrence by Katlin Watson 219
My Special Dad by Jerret Bakker-Orr 219
Stanley Kulikowski by Michael Kulikowski 219
My Grandma by Ethan Trecartin 220
Rob Derosier by Evan Derosier 220
Shawna Ollivier by Hailey Ollivier 220

CHAPTER FIFTEEN: OUR FAITH HERO

Jesus Christ by Tony Fournier 222

OUR GENEROUS SPONSORS

Sponsor Quiz 225

INTRODUCTION

By Matt Amond for
Gerald G. Amond

There are a lot of different kinds of teachers in life. There are of course, teachers who we encounter and learn from at school, who inspire us to dig deeper and communicate their passion for learning every day to us in their classes.

In the last few years I have realized that there are a lot more teachers all around us. They are people who teach us not a specific subject, but the people around us who teach us how to live our life. They provide an example that we can look at and say "That's the kind of man (or woman) that I want to be."

My father has contributed to making this book happen. He was asked to contribute a brief foreword, but he has become very ill with lung and bone cancer, so I will be writing a foreword in his place. I'm happy to do it, because some things I have to say to my father and about my father fit nicely with the theme.

For my whole life my father has not only been my teacher but a teacher of many. Living with dad, it has become my belief that people learn through example and that the best way to get an idea or message across was to live your own life that way as well.

It took me a long time to begin to see the kind of man my father was, which I guess is typical for most kids. But in the last few years, the lessons my father has been teaching me have begun to play a bigger role in my life.

Most of the lessons I've picked up haven't been direct, but things I've pieced together by watching. In the last few months, as dad has become ill, I have seen his years of giving to the community come back to him, as I have seen so many people stopping into the house, sending cards and calling to wish him well.

Dad is, and has been, a teacher to many. As a financial planner, he has helped thousands of people to understand their money, and to understand the future of their money and what it means for their family. As I've grown up and heard more and more about him, a picture of dad as a teacher began to take shape. Like a great teacher, he becomes invested (no pun intended) with his clients and when hard times hits, he is there for them, whether it was for a loss in the family, or to re-evaluate their needs when their situations changed, even if it wasn't the best thing for his business. Dad always knew, and lived and worked, knowing that if he did right by those around him, it would come back to him. This is probably the greatest lesson that he has been able to pass on, and it guides me now every day.

On behalf of dad, I wish you all the best, and I hope that you enjoy the stories assembled here.

Matt

DIRECTOR'S MESSAGE

By **Anna Marie Bitonti**
Director of Education

I am pleased to introduce "You're my Hero™ - Nipissing-Parry Sound Catholic District School Board". This is a tremendous achievement for our young, talented authors. We are happy to share it with our schools and broader community!

With heroes coming from all walks of life, this book is a unique celebration of diversity in family and friendship. Most of all, it is a celebration of our Catholic character and the virtues which are integrated daily into all aspects of learning for our students.

Academically, these young authors, through their eagerness to participate in this book, are a reflection of our Board's commitment to creating high quality learning centres of excellence which are rooted in faith and alive in spirit. Spiritually and morally, through their genuine admiration and respect for their loved ones, these students have shown admirable values vis-à-vis their faith, family, friendship and community. Their stories are an optimistic preview of the fine Catholic graduates and members of society they will surely become.

DIRECTOR`S MESSAGE

I would like to thank all the educators who assisted our authors in this project. Your efforts, guidance and inspiration to these students play an integral role in their learning journey.

We hope that this book will bring smiles to the faces of those who authored it, those who are featured in it, and everyone blessed with reading it.

Congratulations to everyone for this exemplary contribution to our community!

Anna Marie Bitonti
Director of Education

CHAPTER ONE

OUR FAITHFUL HERO

Faith is believing in things when common sense tells you not to.

George Seaton

Father Brian McKee

He was a priest born in North Bay, Ontario. He was my grandmother's brother and my great uncle. His name is Brian McKee and he was the founder of the Flying Father's hockey team.

In 1962, an altar boy in North Bay lost an eye in a hockey accident. Uncle Brian formed a hockey team to play a game to raise money for an operation to fix the boy's eye. That's how the Flying Father's hockey team started. The Flying Fathers won their first game 7 to 3. The priests played lots of tricks on the other team and even sprinkled holy water on the ice to help them win!

The Flying Fathers got really famous and raised over 40 million dollars for different charities and played hockey all over the world. They even got to meet the Pope! Uncle Brian did lots of good by helping poor people and kids. Sadly, in the year 2000, when I was only 3 years old, he passed away. I still like listening to all of the stories about Uncle Brian.

By Joe Cangiano, 10

CHAPTER TWO

HEROES IN OUR SCHOOLS

I like a teacher who gives you something to take home to think about besides homework.

        Lily Tomlin as "Edith Ann"

Coleen Taylor

Mrs. Taylor was an educational assistant and the choir director at St Hubert School for as long as we can remember. She made sure that every student felt welcome and safe at our school. She personally invited all of the new students to our school to come to choir practice so that their voice could be heard. She took time out of her busy schedule to sing and direct our choir, both in and out of school. Mrs Taylor always listened to our stories, gave us advice and offered encouragement when we needed it. She was one of the most special people we have ever met. Just a few short months ago, Mrs Taylor died from a disease called ALS. We miss her terribly and we were very sad for a very long time. When we have mass, we sing songs in memory of Mrs. Taylor and all of the love and kindness she showed us. So, sing loud and long and let the music in you come out because we know Mrs. Taylor is listening.

Grade 3 Class at St. Hubert School

The Kids in the LAC

When they look at me with their smiles, I feel loved and joyful. They make me feel happy inside when I feel blue. These kids are a little different than me and you. They all have special needs. Some are blind and some can't walk. But that's not what makes them special. The special part about these kids in our L.A.C. (Learning Assistance Centre) is that they all have spirit in them. When I give up my recess two times a day, I go to their classroom and play with them.

Whenever I get sad or I've had an argument with one of my friends, these kids are always on my side. Just one hug can change all of my feelings to joy and happiness. Even one smile or a small chuckle can make my day.

The kids in the L.A.C. love songs and stories. They go shopping on Wednesdays and skating on Thursdays and they love it! But most of all, they really love the computer. Their computer has songs that they can listen to like "Old McDonald'.

The Educational Assistants who work with these kids are also my heroes. When I first joined "Care Kids" (a group of friends that meet with the LAC kids each week), the E.A.s taught me everything I needed to know to keep them happy and safe. They have encouraged me to learn how to care for my friends. I hope that one day, when I'm grown up, that I can go back to John XXIII and be a L.A.C. teacher too!

By Courtney Brown, 11

Murray Peavoy

My hero is Murray Peavoy because he is good to our planet. He doesn't use electricity; instead he uses giant solar panels. He has a generator and only uses it if the sun isn't out. He even went one whole year without using the generator. His solar panels are at the side of his house and the energy is stored in his basement.

Mr. Peavoy doesn't have a heater or air conditioner. He has a wood stove (fireplace) that he uses for heat. I've only been to his house once during the winter, but I'm sure he just opens the door in the summer if he's hot. Mr. Peavoy even pumps his own water from a well.

My hero is a retired teacher who taught at F.J. McElligott High School in Mattawa. He taught my dad, my uncles and my aunts. He taught physical education, math and science.

Murray Peavoy is a hero because he has taken the steps to help save our planet even though it means more work. If more people did this, it would help save our planet and everyone on it.

By Jennilee Peplinskie, 11

Joyce Daniels

My hero is my special educational worker and my special friend. She is really kind and nice to me. She helps me learn at school and has helped me get into city sports like hockey and baseball. She has taught me to be a kind person and to always do my best at whatever I do. She is my hero because she has helped me grow up into a young, responsible adult. She has been my educational worker since I was 6 years old.

When I first met Joyce I was very shy. I then got to know her and now I am so happy to be working with her. Joyce takes the time to help out with my school work and my work from English. She also takes me out to places around the community. Joyce is very special to me and I'm very lucky to have a hero like Joyce in my life.

By Corey Fulford, 13

Mrs. Hegyi

My hero is someone who is always willing to help me no matter what. She has made me a better person and has made me more confident with who I am. She has inspired me in many ways and she is a very caring, loving person. No matter what happens, I know I can count on her for anything. My hero is my teacher, Mrs. Hegyi.

One of the reasons my teacher is an important person to me is because she cares about her students very much. For instance, I was never very good in math until this year, when she started math help sessions on Tuesdays and Thursdays. Ever since I started going to math help, my marks have improved a lot and I feel more confident during math class.

Every day I look forward to her classes because she makes the lessons entertaining and interesting. She is an organized person. She has a lot of patience and she has a good sense of humour. She interacts well with her students, has an amazing personality and understands her students well. Overall, I think it is because she loves her job that she is so great at it!

Mrs. Hegyi has inspired me to achieve more, to be more helpful to others, to put more effort into my work and to get help when it is needed. She has made me a better problem solver. I sometimes get into little fights or disagreements. She taught me to talk it out and not keep it all bottled up inside; that way, you don't become enemies with the other person.

Mrs. Hegyi means a lot to me and I will never forget all the things she has taught me and how she has changed my life. Most importantly, I will never forget her as I begin my journey through high school. Thank you, Mrs. Hegyi, for all you have done!

By Vanessa Amyotte, Grade 8

Mme Klein et Matthew Leblond

J'ai deux héros. Un est un ami et l'autre est une madame. Les deux m'ont aidé dans mes premières années à l'école.

Mme Klein m'a aidé le plus. Elle est une enseignante à St.Theresa, une école catholique. Quand j'étais petit, en JK/SK, j'avais un ami, seulement un, parce que j'avais un problème, ma colère. Mme Klein m'a aidé. Maintenant, je suis gentil et c'est à cause d'elle.

J'ai un ami qui s'appelle Matthew. Il a un besoin en écriture. Il est le seul garçon qui veut jouer avec moi. Il a 10 ans et est en cinquième année. Il est un bon ami et il est aussi un héros dans mon coeur. Je veux lui dire merci!

Mme Klein et mon ami Matthew m'ont aidé parce qu'ils m'ont donné la chance d'être aimé et d'avoir des amis.

Merci pour tout ce que vous avez fait pour moi.... vous êtes tous les deux des héros dans mon coeur. Merci!!!

Par Owen Joiner, 10

Mr. Jacques

I think a hero in our school is Mr. Jacques. When the ball goes on the roof, he gets it. He opens stuff. If it gets stuck, he opens it. He keeps the school super clean and he washes the desks for us. That's why I think he is my hero.

By Jo-Anna Fleury, 7

Dione Turgeon

Il y a une femme qui joue un rôle très important dans ma vie. Elle a 34 ans et elle est mon enseignante, Mme Turgeon.

Elle est ma héroïne parce qu'elle m'enseigne. Elle enseigne très, très bien. Elle m'aide à lire, écrire et avec les mots. Elle est aussi ma héroïne parce qu'elle aide ma grande soeur. Elle est très, très bonne à ça. Elle est aussi ma héroïne parce qu'elle m'aime de la même façon que mes parents. Cette femme est très gentille. Je l'aime beaucoup. Ce rôle est très important dans ma vie.

By Cathy Shaw, 7

Madame Turgeon

Il y a une femme importante dans ma vie et elle est une enseignante. Elle a des idées intéressantes. Elle est Mme Turgeon. Elle est gentille. Il y a 18 personnes dans sa classe, 10 troisième années, et 8 quatrième années. Toutes les personnes sont des amis.

Elle a des cheveux courts et elle est belle. Elle porte toujours des chaussures à talons hauts. Elle a des cheveux bruns. Elle utilise beaucoup de dictionnaires. Elle est gentille comme j'ai dit, mais je le dit encore.

Elle entre toute la classe dans des concours et toute la classe a de bonnes notes sur les bulletins comme un A+ ou B+, pas de C. C'est mon histoire.

By N. Paquet, 9

Miss Clark

Miss Clark is my hero. She is bright and she is very intelligent. When I am at school it feels like she is in my family. Miss Clark also has really good teaching skills.

She is very, very, very talented. She is brave and helpful. When she teaches math and when I am stuck, she is there for me.

Miss Clark has blond hair, blue eyes and loves to click her heels on the ground. She is the best teacher in the world and that's why she is my hero!

By Lia Castiglione, 8

On behalf of the Students of the
Nipissing – Parry Sound Catholic District School Board,
Gerry and Barry would like to acknowledge:

THE PRINCIPALS

THE SECRETARIAL STAFF

THE ADMIN STAFF

THE CUSTODIAL AND MAINTENANCE STAFF

THE BOARD

THE BOARD STAFF

THE TRUSTEES AND

THE PARENTS

MERCI!
MIIGWECH!
THANK YOU!

*Achiu • Arigato • Danke • Dank u
Dyakooyu • Dziekuje • Gratia • Grazie • Grazzii • Hvala
Kiitos • Kinanaskomitinawaw • Komapsumnida
Koszonom • Mahalo • Muchas gracias • Multumesc • Obrigado
Tack • Tujechhe • Xie xie*

TRUSTEES

Jacques Begin   Shawn Fitzsimmons

Don Houle   Judy Manitowabi

Barbara Mc Cool   Frank O'Hagan

SENIOR ADMINISTRATION

Anna Marie Bitonti
Director of Education

Grace Barnhardt
Superintendent of Business & Treasurer

Joanne Bénard
Superintendent of Education

Msgr. Norm Clement
Board Chaplain

Karen Fabbro-Cobb
Senior Education Official

Paula Mann
Senior Education Official

CORPUS CHRISTI

Callahan, Kathy
Charles, Sandra
Courchesne, Melanie
Fitzgerald, Rose
Hlusek, Michelle
Hoover, Rosemary
Jerome, Shannon
Klein, Cathy
Renton, Carole Anne
Schlueting, Lori
Soule, Sandra
Van Beek, Marianne

JOHN XXIII

Barton, Suzanne
Beaulieu, Tanya
Bernardi, Lynne
Boucher, Mark
Charette, Suzanne
Chaylt, Diane
Cirullo, Lise
Coulombe, Brigitte
Daniels, Joyce
Fitzgerald, Wallace
Galan, Tracie
Gravelle, Tammy
Guillemette, John
Huywan, Audette
Luesby, Cindy
Mallinson, Lorraine
Paquette, Leoni
Prescott, Carol
Selin, Denise
Tancredi, Charles
Terbovc, Pierrette
Vezina, Patti

OUR LADY OF FATIMA

Boulet, Eileen
Castiglione, Nathalie
Caven, Tara
Chenier, Diane
Conlon, Rosemary
D'Agostino, Anthony
Fava, Elizabeth
Gauthier, Maria
Gravelle, Patricia
Greenwood, Jerry
Jacques, Jerry
Lafond, Samantha
Mallinson, Lorraine
MacLeod, Christopher
Pangos, Fiona
Price, Peter
Suszter, Rhonda
Tarini, Laura
Warman, Carolyn
White, Beverly

OUR LADY OF SORROWS

Allaire, Nancy
Arcand-Horner, Sylvie
Cosgrove, Sharon
De Jourdan, Emily
Desormiers, Caroline
Ducharme, Dan
Fisher, Candace
Gerrard, Gerry
Giandomenico, Flo
Giandomenico, Theresa
Horner, Mark
Horner, Tisha
Kleinhuis, Steve
Levac, Monique
Malette, Stacey
Martin, Jovette
McLeod, Darlene
Primeau, Paul
Rothwell, Anna Marie
Smilie, Vicki
Sullivan, Maggie
Walsh, Stacey
Willemsen, Mary
Wilson, Colette

SACRED HEART

Allaire, Kim
Aquino, Nathalie
Bale, Allen
Blais, Renée
Charette, Suzanne
Chaylt, Diane
Coulombe, Marc
Fitzgerald, Wally
Gauthier, Kim
Ledoux, Pat
MacDonnell, Kathleen
Madigan, Shanna
Sayer-Whittet, Kim
Seguin, Dan
Stevens, Sacha
Storie, Kathy
Thayer, Micheline
Tignanelli, Josie
Wilson, Colette
Zimbalatti, Sandro

ST. ALEXANDER

Bailey, Michelle
Buckley, Anne
Chassé, Tammy
Clark, Kerri
Coulombe, Marc
Dicks, Cheryl
Emond, MacDonald
Emond-D'Agostino, Rhonda
Fior, Maureen
Forest, Mary
Gal, Anne
Graham, Cathy
Gribbons-Robillard, Audrey
Laperriere, Julie
Mann, Paula
Mantha, Linda
Mechefske, Sandra
Moore, Joanne
Parker, Caroline
Pavone, Erin
Pigeau, Anthony
Saunders, Nancy
Shago, Nolana
Shoppoff, Susan
Spiess, Theresa
Sunstrum, Ross
Van De Wal, Giuliana
Vigna, Sonia
Wilson, Corinne
Wilson, Kristin

ST. FRANCIS

Aquino, Nathalie
Aube, Ginette
Boissonneault, Roxanne
Champagne, Claude
Charette, Suzanne
Charland, Josée
Goldthorp, Carolyn
Goulet, Kayla
Greenwood, Gerry
King, Josée
Machac, Elizabeth
Madigan, Shanna
Morawski, Tracy
Perrault, Janet
Renaud, Patricia
Van Schaayk, Sue

ST. HUBERT

Bennison, Charlene
Carreiro, Elizabeth
Courchesne, Steve
Dietrich, Diane
Doucette, Twyla
Falconi, Gloria
Falconi, Nicki
Forsyth, Chris
Francis, Nancy
Gaudaur, Bernie
Hrbolich, Maureen
Kaspardlov, Caroline
Lebel, Robert
Lingenfelter, Peter
MacLeod, Elizabeth
McCharles, Patricia
McCutcheon, Bryan
McParland, Gary
Mitchell, Karen
Nidd, Cheryl
Norman, Alanna
Pavone, Rob
Perreault, Marc
Pigeau, Suzanne
Prior, Mary Ann
Rose, Brenda
Stott, Candy
Surtees, Sarah
Tayler, Erin
Vaillancourt, Brenda

ST. JOSEPH

Beauchamp, Jennifer
Cazabon, Richard
Crockett, Ritchie
Dunkley, Erin
Fiorino, Marco
Korosec, Sue
Price, Lynn
Raymond, Ron
Savard, Christina
Shaver, Jocelyn
Tignanelli, Marcello
Valiquette, Maureen
Van Beek, Marianne
Wall, Diane

ST. VICTOR

Blanchard, Melodie
Cotnam, Angela
Dumont, Shelley
Dupuis, Gilles
Houston, Karen
Konkal, Loni
Lamirante, Danielle
Lefebvre, Robert
O'Grady, Connie
Verardi-Campoverde, Cathy
Whalley, Chantal
Zimbalatti, Sandro

To: Our Teachers
Our Educational Assistants
Our Faculties
Our Guidance Counsellors
Our Administration Staff
Our Custodial Staff
Our Boards of Education

Thank You!

Heartfelt thanks go out to our TROOPS, VETERANS and their FAMILIES

from the team at
You`re My Hero™ *Books Ltd.*

CHAPTER THREE

OUR FRIENDS

Friends are God's way of taking care of us.
Marlene Dietrich

An Unlikely Friend

It was my grade six year. I was the only one out of my little circle of friends that was going to another school to take French Immersion. I was scared. Seated in the front row of my French class, I kept my eyes downcast, wishing to God that I had waited to switch schools until the following year. Someone had come and sat in the desk beside me. I discreetly peeked over and realized it was one of the people I loathed the most from my previous school. She had bullied me off and on for the past two years and the last thing I wanted was for this person to sit beside me. But there was something different about her and the more I stared at her, the more I realized she was just as scared as I was. She caught my stare and sheepishly asked me if she and I could be friends. Neither of our friends had come to the school, so it was just her and I. I was dumbfounded. While I was struggling for an answer, I was thinking in my head, 'Don't do it! It's another one of her bullying tactics. Don't do it!' Reluctantly, I said yes and that day was the start of one of the greatest friendships I have ever had.

For the past six years I have been going through my own trials and tribulations, dealing with self-destructive actions that could have potentially left me for dead. She was one of the first people that sat and listened to the problems I had. She loved me enough to stay with me and be my friend, even when I wasn't the friendliest. She was the first one to get after me about my self-destructive behaviour and to get some professional help. She's strong when you need her to be. She isn't too afraid to be vulnerable. In my opinion, that is one of the bravest things that a person could ever be. Though she and I are apart now (I have moved away), we still are really close and I find myself missing her crazy ways and contagious optimism. She is my hero and my best friend because of extraordinary heroic efforts to save a life from a burning building. It's because, in her little ways, she changed my life.

By Stephanie Schmidt

Alyssa Thibault

Alyssa Thibault is my hero because one day in my life, she was there. She was the one. She had the courage to talk to me, walk with me, play with me and even be my best friend. That one day was the best day in my life.

We told stories of our lives and we found out that we were to be friends. She asked me, "Why aren't you playing with your friends?" and I said, "Because there is no one that is my type." She was shocked. She looked around and said, "I will play with you."

We went off to play and a girl named Grace came and said, "Can I play?" It was like a miracle. That is how we met and are still friends. Then one day, she came to my house and gave me an invitation. I did not know what it was. I looked at it and she was moving to Aurora. It was a goodbye party. I did not want her to go, not one bit. The party was great. It was a good idea. When it was done, I never, ever saw her again.

Megan Stickle, 10

Alexis Meecham

Alexis is my hero because when my father, Ross Swayne, passed away, I was crying and crying and I couldn't stop. The first person I called was Alexis. She understands me. She helped me stop crying. I invited her over. I told her what happened. She knew how it felt because her dad almost died in his car accident.

Then we played and we laughed. She made me feel a bit better. She comforted me and I comforted her when she and her dad, Jody, got into that car accident. When that happened, Alexis was very brave. She's still very brave, let me tell you! We're both sticking together so we can become even more brave because we're best friends. Nothing can tear us apart! I'm like her sister. I help her and she helps me.

By Olivia Côté, 8

Kurtis David

Kurtis is my best, best friend. The reason why he is my friend is because when I found out that I was allergic to peanuts and nuts, Kurtis was the first to know and told the whole grade one class. Not only is he my friend, but I'm his best friend too. The reason I'm his best friend is because on my second day at G. H. Ferguson School, Kurtis fell and hurt himself very badly. The recess supervisor, my mom, told me to take Kurtis inside to the office. On the seventh day, I got a big paper cut. The teacher, Mrs. Morgan, told Kurtis to take me to the office. That's the way Kurtis is my hero.

Brady Boileau, 11

My Friends

In 2006, my mom told me that we were moving. I was really happy about moving. Then my mom told me that because we were moving, we had to change schools. My jaw dropped to the floor. I said, "Do we have to move?" she said, "yes". So I ran to my room with hatred in my heart. I kept asking myself, "Do I have to change schools?"

April came strolling along and the next thing you know we were out of the house. We started unpacking. There were only three bedrooms. My parents have their own room, my brother has his own room and now, I have to share a room with my sister! Since we lived out in West Ferris, we were supposed to go to the school nearest to my house. We would start the next September because my school, John XXIII, bussed me and my two siblings there until the end of the year. It wouldn't matter to my brother. He was graduating from grade 8 and my sister would be at a new school for only one year since she was in grade 7. I would be there for two years.

I started Grade 5. I went to school and the principal showed me around. The first two people I met were Shannon and Kristen. I felt so happy I met them. The bell rang. It was time to go inside the classes. When I got there, the desks were in pairs of two. I sat with Megan Rice. I was so happy. I made friends at a new school and I will never forget what happened. I will always keep that moment in my heart.

By Chelsea Dietrich, 12

Kelsey Michaud

My hero's name is Kelsey Michaud. I chose to write about Kelsey because she was my first friend I met when I started school. In Junior Kindergarten, whenever it was playtime, we would always play together. We would always finger paint and then we would give our pictures to each other and then take them home. I remember last year we went to the kindergarten room for a day and we finger painted for about an hour. We had a lot of fun playing together.

Kelsey was the first person I had a sleepover with. We were four years old at the time. We had played for a while with this new toy dog she had gotten. When it came time for bed, we slept on her pull out couch with lots of blankets. Kelsey woke up before me and then we ate some cereal for breakfast. Kelsey still has a picture of us in bed.

But Kelsey moved 20 minutes away about five years ago, so I only see her at school. We still have a lot of fun. In school we sit beside each other, so we talk all the time. At recess we amuse ourselves by playing games like four square, skipping, bump and spud. Sometimes, we just talk.

Kelsey has been my friend for about eight years and I'm sure she will be for eight more. I really appreciate her being my friend and staying by my side for all these years. I'm sure she feels the same way!

By Julia Anne Harkness, 11

Travis Lemieux

My hero is Travis because when we first met each other we became friends. Why? Every time I am sad he comes and says, "Don't worry. Don't be sad, Jaydan."

By Jayden McLeod, 6

Katie Svenson
(A Girl with Dreams)

An equestrian at heart, Katie Svensson is one of my best friends. At the age of 16, she inspired me to become a vegetarian. The reason that I nominated her as my hero is because she does the most intense things that I dream I could do.

One of the heroic things that she did was try to help prevent a horse, Chance, from dying of colic. Colic is the number one reason horses die each year. Their intestines twist so they roll around to make their stomach stop hurting. What the horses don't know is that it'll just make the pain a lot worse. Katie tried her best by encouraging Chance to get up, but he would just fall back down. Sadly, the colic was too bad and the vet had to put him down. I bet that it took a lot of courage for her to help Chance, then to have to finally say goodbye, forever. Someday, I wish I can make an animal comfortable during its last minutes of living.

This past September, my friends and I went to Palgrave, Ontario, to watch Katie compete in the Trillium Championships. She had to jump four feet while riding Whiskey over some intimidating coloured jumps. I think that she was really brave. It takes a lot of guts to go in shows, especially when there are hundreds of people watching. I guess that doing that on Whiskey really boosted her confidence. She would die for that horse.

I'm so proud to be a part of Katie's life. I love getting her advice, being around her when she's being cantankerous and I'm so glad that she's there for me when I need her the most. I hope that someday I'll grow up to be a hero just like her.

By Vicky Gorecki, 13

Ken Downton

Kenny Downton is my and my mom's friend and has been for five years. He's my hero because he is in the Canadian Forces and he went to war for six months in Afghanistan to help our country. He left at the beginning of August 2007 and came back February 2008. He is 40 years old and he's been working for the Canadian Forces for I don't know how long.

Kenny and his family lived a block from my house. When he was still here, we had a party and we went to The Moose Restaurant on Main Street. We went there for the wings. We had a surprise 40th birthday party for Kenny and my uncle at Peachey's Restaurant. We were there for so long that I lost track of time.

Kenny thinks of me while he's working. Kenny sent me a parcel from Afghanistan with a shirt that says, "If you can't stand the heat, we can!". He also sent me a keychain that has a frozen scorpion in it. Kenny sent all my cousins a parcel too.

Kenny has been almost everywhere in the world. He's been to Iraq, Egypt, Russia, Paris, Germany and so many other places. Kenny is my hero because he went to war for six months. He missed his daughter's birthday and Christmas for our country. If you knew him he would be your hero too!

By Patrick St. Louis, 11

Caitlin Howard

My hero is Caitlin. She is a great friend. Caitlin is my hero because she is always there for me. For example, when I am lonely, she is always there to play. Caitlin has brown hair and green eyes. She loves to read and write. Caitlin is a great friend. She helps me because she really cares. She has courage, leadership and strength. Caitlin is my hero.

By Daniela Pettela, 8

Triple A Trophy & Awards

2213 Trout Lake Rd.
North Bay, Ont., P1B 7S3
Ph:705-474-2168 Fax:705-474-2139

email : leslie@tripleatrophy.ca
www.tripleatrophy.ca

Customized Engraving
Awards & Promotional
Specialists

Our One Price Awards
NOW
Include Engraving & Setup

Leslie Cerisano

Yes! Employment Services

Oui! Services à l'emploi

We provide services to help individuals find
meaningful employment, return to school,
access training and discover
their true potential.

We are a community organization
working for our community.

149 Main Street East, North Bay, ON P1B 1A9
Phone: 705-476-3234 • Fax: 705-476-9302
www.yesnorthbay.com • info@yesnorthbay.com

CHAPTER FOUR

OUR DADS

My father used to play with my brother and me in the yard. Mother would come out and say, "You're tearing up the grass." "We're not raising grass," Dad would reply. "We're raising boys."

Harmon Killebrew

Mark Hummel
(My Star Hero)

A lot of dads are too strict or too fun, but not my dad. He has his rules but knows how to have fun at the same time. He also keeps me healthy. We only go out to a restaurant about once a week. He also has a sweet tooth like me. We love candy and chocolate and we drown our pancakes in syrup. Whenever my mom goes out with her friends, we rent a movie and buy candy and chips!

My dad works at Boart Longyear. They make drills and other machines. He gave me a tour of it once. It's really cool! I always watch hockey with him. Although we cheer for different teams, it doesn't make a difference. He makes me laugh a lot and I mean a lot! He lets me shovel the driveway and rake the leaves with him. I always watch him barbecue. He makes awesome hamburgers.

In the summer, we go on bike rides to keep us active. My dad loves to play baseball with me ever since I got my new mitt. Sometimes, he plays badminton and volleyball with me too. I love going grocery shopping at No Frills and just plain shopping at Wal-Mart with him.

My dad doesn't like to spend a lot of money on anything. For example, if there was a milk jug for $1.99 and a bag of milk for $1.00, he would by the bag of milk. Don't ask me why, though I would probably do the same. I just don't get it now. My dad is my role model. He is my star I look up to.

Even though I disagree with him sometimes, I still love him very much. My dad is my hero, in general, for everything he does!

By Taylor Hummel, 10

Brad Burden

My hero cannot be found in movies or in comics. My hero is a little more real; well, was real. He was always waiting for me at the end of the driveway with his cup of coffee and a cigarette in the corner of his mouth. He would give me a great big hug and say, "Good morning, Scooter!" He kept a roof over my head no matter how much he had to travel. We always waited at the airport for him to come home from work. He was there for me when my grandpa died. He took me to my first basketball game. He showed me how to skate and how to play my first guitar chord. He was there for me during the good times and the bad. My hero is my dad, Brad Burden. R.I.P. Dad.

By Harley Burden, 13

Jean-Marc Leblond

Bonjour, je m'appelle Matthew et je veux te parler de mon héros. Mon héros est un homme qui a risqué sa vie pour un animal. L'animal est un chien et il a un an en années de chien.

Un jour, mon héros a répondu a un appel de feu qui était chez mon voisin. C'était un gros feu, très, très, très grand. Mon héros est allé dans le feu. Sa mission était de sauver un chien parce que l'homme a seulement un membre dans sa famille et c'est le chien.

Il a combattu le feu comme c'était la fin du monde. Il a pu attraper le chien quand l'alarme a sonné et mon héros a dû se sauver de la maison qui était en feu avant qu'elle explose. Il a complété sa mission.

Matthew Leblond, 10

NB: Je t'aime papa!!

Chris Galema

'Doctor' is a word that you hear a lot in the English language. "Oh, I need a doctor," some people will say, dramatically, as they hold their precious little knee. 'Doctor, doctor' jokes are some of the best jokes in the books. But have you ever thought of the true meaning of doctor. They don't just think of you, but everyone: their family, their friends, their patients. Maybe even aliens!

My dad is a doctor and that's one thing I admire about him. A second reason is because he's always there to say, 'Here, have one of these,' when I'm sick. And third, he's not just a doctor, he's also a dad. He manages to squeak in some time to have fun with me and my brothers. My dad isn't always at his office. He still takes time to skate, play outside, play Warhammer or play video games. He's always there for me when I need him the most and we have a lot of fun together.

We all hate having to get needles and having to drink gross pulpy medicine, but do you really think that your doctor is trying to hurt you? He's only trying to make you feel better or prevent you from getting sick. He says it's sort of fun trying to make kids or adults feel better. That's one reason why I admire my dad.

When I'm sick, I actually consider myself lucky because I don't have to drive into town to a doctor's office. My dad just gives me the medicine I need to feel better. His first priority when I'm sick is to make me feel better, even when he has something important to do. I love my dad a lot.

So as you can see, I love my dad very much. He cares for aliens. We found a UFO in our backyard and we're keeping it hostage!!!

By Matthew Peterson-Galema, 11

Fred Cormier

For four of the five years that I have played soccer, my dad has volunteered to be my coach. He has taken two coaching courses so he would be able to follow me to the next level.

His volunteer work even extends beyond me. When my mom needs help with something, she can always rely on him to be there for her. Each year that she needed help to set up the Halloween display at the complex, he made himself available to her. He has also been involved with each of the three Christmas floats for my mom's work. This past Christmas, he realized how important the Santa photo display was to my mom so he gave suggestions and helped move furniture to get it set up and ready. Also, when my mom volunteered for the Relay for Life event, he didn't hesitate to lend a hand putting up the tents, providing a heater and setting up the banner.

The times he shines most are when he is helping out friends and family. With a simple phone call, he is available for a safe ride home, to fix a flat tire, to help with renovations, provide carpentry tips or even just to be there for a buddy. All of these acts of kindness and generosity are done without any expectations of a single thing in return.

I will have a lot of teachers in my life and I'd like to consider my dad as one. He teaches me how to ride the four-wheeler and snowmobile and how to improve my soccer techniques. He teaches me how to cook and fish. He's also helped me with my swimming and diving.

Ivan's Restaurant
A North Bay Tradition
The Original Ted's since 1945

Take Out or Eat In
(705) 474-2150
1867 O'Brien North Bay

These are all great for everyday use but the character skills he has passed on to me are the ones that will make me a better person. They are also what truly makes my dad my hero.

Kaitlyn Cormier, 12

Chris McDonell

My dad is a forester and he helps the world. He helps the world by saving trees and not killing them. He helps the world by planting trees so we have more fresh air. My dad also goes into the forest and looks at animals. And most importantly, he's my dad.

By Kara McDonell, 8

Kurtis Summers

When I was two years old, I was at Grandma's house. In the back yard, she has stairs going into another part of her garden. My sister and I were playing Follow the Leader and she was the leader. I was following her. She went down the stone stairs. I tried to follow her but I lost my balance and fell on my head. I started bleeding and crying.

My daddy and grandma heard me and came running and picked me up, but they couldn't tell where all the blood was coming from. They got into the car and brought me to St. Joseph's Hospital. When they got in, they were in such a panic that they forgot that St. Joseph's Hospital didn't have an emergency department, so they had to get in the car again and drive to another hospital, the Civic.

When we got in, the nurse recognized daddy and grandma and took me in right away. They cleaned most of the blood off and daddy cleaned some of the blood off his shirt. They figured out that the blood was coming from my forehead - the middle of my forehead! They put some stitches in and we all went home. When we got there, my mommy was there with Hannah and she came up and gave me a big hug. I was all right. Daddy was my hero because he picked me up and got in the car and brought me to the hospital without panicking. Well, he did panic a little when he went to the wrong hospital, but that's okay. He was very brave to be able to do that and I love him.

By Isabelle Summers, 10

Mark DiLello

My hero is my dad. In the summer, we usually play catch. We throw it to each other and sometimes I miss it. Sometimes I don't. When I miss it, I have to go all the way down the road to get it. When I was little, we play-wrestled. He picked me up with his legs. We go skating and play road hockey sometimes. We play video games and I always beat him.

My dad is always funny at the dinner table. We're always happy. He helps me with science and helps me when I'm hurt. We go to the golf course and the driving range. He hits the ball hard. When the ball curves, he calls it a banana!! It's funny! We always watch hockey and baseball games and soccer games. He plays baseball with me and he is my coach for soccer. He's the best coach ever! He plays board games with me and my mom. My dad is playful and teaches me how to play soccer. We play 21 or Pig. We love each other and play a lot. That's why my dad is my hero!

By Aidan DiLello, 9

Stephan Michaud

My hero is my daddy becuase my daddy is in Saskatoon. My daddy is in Saskatoon because he is trying to earn money for food. My daddy is very brave to be in Saskatoon because there are barely any trees there. My daddy is going to quit so he doesn't have to move there. My daddy is bald and has a little hair at the back of his head. I love my daddy!

By Alia Michaud, 8

Vito Castiglione

My dad works really hard to earn money for our house and food. My dad has to go places for meetings out of town.

My dad has black hair and a little bit of gray hair. He likes wearing brown boots.

My hero is brave because he faces his fears. My dad has strength, leadership and courage. I love my dad. He teaches me a lot. My dad goes away for soccer too. My dad helps out with hockey. My dad is fantastic!

Kara Castiglione, 9

Shadow Commanda

Shadow is my daddy. He loves to go shopping to look for games for my brother and I for our computer. He has black hair. His favourite colour is white and his favourite dog is a black lab.

My daddy loves me and my family lots. My daddy made me a rink. He made my brother and I a fort but it melted so we couldn't play inside of it.

My daddy is my hero because he helps me with my homework. When I'm stuck, he helps me.

By Jamie Commanda, 9

Jon Cerisano

My hero is my dad. He is old. He helps me with my homework. I love my dad!!!

By Connor Cerisano, 6

Ryan Fuerth

My dad is my hero. His name is Ryan. He helps me with my homework and he helps me catch butterflies. He loves me and he works very hard for me to see him. I love my dad.

By Bella Fuerth, 6

Mark Cicciarelli

My hero is my dad because he saved me from an icicle falling on my head.

By Nicholas Cicciarelli, 5

Rodney St. Denis

Mon héros est mon papa parce qu'il a sauvé ma maman. Mon papa a sauvé ma maman d'un ours.

By Claudia Heffern

Sam Jackson
A Guardian Angel for Logan

Since I was a little girl, my dream had always been to have a child of my own. My wish came true on September 8th, 2006 when I gave birth to a beautiful baby boy named Logan. What made this day even more special was that my parents were able to make the trip from North Bay to Montreal to witness the birth of their grandchild. The thing I remember the most about Logan's birthday is seeing my father, my hero, hold him and cry. It is a sight that will forever be engraved in my memory and little did I know that it would be the first and last time my son would be held by his grandfather.

My father, Sam Jackson, is the man who helped me become the woman I am today. He taught me how to throw a ball, to fight for what I believe in, to laugh even when I wished I could cry, to find the good in people and to try to make the best out of the obstacles I faced on a daily basis. Because he meant so much to me, I couldn't wait for him to meet my son, to watch him grow and to instill the same great values in Logan that he had in me. I just knew how much fun they would have together.

Three weeks after Logan was born, I got a phone call from my mom telling me I had better get to North Bay quickly as they didn't think my dad would make it through the week. He had been sick but we didn't realize just how ill he really was. I could hear by the tone of my mom's voice that things weren't going to be okay. I made it to the hospital on time to say goodbye to my dad. At this point, he wasn't really able to speak and slept most of the time because of the high dosage of medication. I sat beside him and held his hand while I held my son in my other arm. It's then that my father opened his eyes and said: "Hi Baby Logan". My family and I just sat there speechless as my dying father stared into the eyes of my newborn son and gave him one last smile. It lasted for only a minute and then my father closed his eyes again.

Those were the last words I heard him speak. He passed away a few hours later.

I was so angry when my father died and I just couldn't understand why this was happening to us. He was so young and suffered so much, it just wasn't fair. I was crying in the hallway of the hospital, when Sherry, a nurse in the palliative care unit came to console me. I'll never forget what she said: "Sylvie, I am so honoured that I was able to be a part of your father's journey." Wow, she was so right.

Although our time together was cut short, I was so blessed to have had him as a father. More importantly, it is at that moment that I realized that life had just given my son his own personal guardian angel. I could swear that, when I rock my son at night, I can hear my father sing and as I put my Logan to bed, I know he will be fine because he has his Poppa to watch over him. I couldn't have asked for a more precious gift!

by Sylvie Jackson

EDITOR'S NOTE:

This beautiful and touching story was originally supposed to be in our first book, YOU'RE MY HERO™ - NORTH BAY. Due to a mistake on our part the story was missed.

Since Louise Jackson, wife of Sam, was a teacher in the Catholic school system, we wanted to take this opportunity to honour Sam, Sylvie, Logan and Louise Jackson.

J.C. Desbiens

My hero is my dad. He helps me when I'm hurting. My dad is the best!

By Joshua Desbiens, 6

Everyday Heroes

Cementation is proud to be the first company to sponsor the *You're My Hero* project in North Bay. In our company we have many employees who exercise courageous leadership in safety. These employees are our everyday heroes because by promoting safe work practices they prevent injuries and ultimately save lives, and what could be more heroic than that.

We believe in everyday heroes.

Cementation
WE BUILD MINES

www.cementation.ca • 705.472.3381

EVANS BERTRAND HILL WHEELER
ARCHITECTURE INC

528 Cassells Street
North Bay, Ontario P1B 3Z7
T 705 472-0890 • F 705 472-2486
www.ebhwarchitecture.ca

mitchellarchitects

124A Main Street East
North Bay, ON
705-474-3250
www.mitchellarchitects.ca

LAROCQUE ELDER ARCHITECTS INC.

188 FIFTH AVENUE EAST
NORTH BAY, ONTARIO
705 497 9191

Northern Renovation Centre

71 Lakeshore Dr.
North Bay
475-1472

SPILCHUK

RENOVATIONS • DESIGN • CONTRACTING

TIM SPILCHUK

705-495-5324

BUILDING YOUR VISION

CHAPTER FIVE

OUR MOMS

A mother is a person who seeing there are only four pieces of pie for five people, promptly announces she never did care for pie.

Tenneva Jordan

Patricia Sutherland

I have been told, time and time again, how mature I am for my age. Sure, this is gained from experience but if these people met my mom and sat down and talked to her, they would see where I gained these traits. She taught me empathy and understanding without teaching me what they were called. She taught me many things that I never knew had names.

I have a terrible memory, even at 17. I can remember day-to-day things but I have difficulty remembering the details of my past. She remembers what I never possibly could and tells my stories as though they are all, individually, unforgettable. Even more, she makes me feel unforgettable. The things that are important to me are just as important to her. If I could break off a piece of my mom's spirit without diminishing it in anyway, I would share it with everyone. I would share her pureness of heart and goodness with anyone who may need it.

As I grow older, I can only wish to possess all of the qualities that my hero does. I believe she has taught me things that take people lifetimes to grasp. My hero is my mom, and I hope I can one day understand everything about her that I find mysterious.

By Dawn Lamothe, 17

Teena Cross

She is the inspiration in my life. She's taught me to keep moving on, no matter how tough the situation is. Four years ago, my mom went back to school to get a better job. I was okay with that. The first year went by. My sister and I started getting bored. If I wasn't at school I was at home alone with my sister. I remember going to sleep, listening to typing on the computer, and waking up to the same sound.

In 2004, my mom left for six weeks on a placement in Kingston. Me and my sister stayed with my older cousin. I was lonely. In 2006, my mom left on another placement to Val Caron for training to be a corrections officer. My grandma took care of us. My mom called us every night after her training and supper. Sometimes, she called us in the morning before school.

After 4 years of hard work, my mom graduated from Nipissing University with a Bachelor of Arts degree. One week before that, my mom graduated from Val Caron. I was so proud of my mom. My mom now works at the North Bay jail as a corrections officer.

By Kelsey Michaud, 11

Michelle Ricciuto

My mom is a wonderful woman. I sometimes call her 'wonder mommy' because when she comes home from work, she makes dinner, puts away clothes, does the dishes, folds more laundry and then gets time to sit down. My mom also works full time, so I would like to give her credit because I think she thinks nobody cares. Truly everybody that lives in my house does care but we don't give her credit. I feel bad so I am dedicating this story to her. I'll bet you every mother comes home and does what my mom does, but not the way my mom does it.

To begin with, she gave birth to me. She also puts a roof over my head. She is loving, caring and helpful when you need advice about things that you cannot discuss with your father.

I think all moms are meant to be helpful and not enjoy doing all that they do. But really, if they asked the children to do it, it's either not the right way or just wrong. I truly do love my mother and I'm writing this to show her that I do notice everything that she does and that I am now giving her the credit that she deserves. I'm sorry if I do not point out everything you do but I notice it and always remember that I care.

Mom, you are loving because when you come home from work, you make sure you give me a big hug. You are caring because you care about me and my brother's health and education. You are joyful because you are fun. Even though you are usually busy, you still find a way to keep me happy.

By Victoria Ricciuto, 12

Wendy Aiton

My mom's name is Wendy. She's short. She has blond hair and blue eyes. My mom mostly lets me do my homework but she sometimes helps. When I was sick, my teacher had to send some homework home so I could catch up. My mom encouraged me to finish it.

My mom is brave because when there is a spider on the floor, she picks it up and puts it outside so it won't die. She is also brave because she was in a car accident and she had to go to the hospital. Her arm was broken but she didn't complain. I really love my mom.

By Melanie Aiton, 9

Tracy Godon

My mom is there whenever I need her, through the rough times and the good times. Whenever I am stuck on a word for reading, she helps me. When we went to Warren to go horseback riding, she was there to help me when I was scared.

One time, my mom took me to McDonald's for ice cream. It was only her and me. I had a soft ice cream cone dipped in chocolate. My mom had a plain, soft ice cream cone. This was the best time ever. I wish we could do it again.

By Corey John Stone, 12

Chantalle Cardelli

My mom is Chantalle Cardelli and she has brownish, yellowish hair which is very short. She has brownish, greenish eyes. She wears glasses and she loves to work.

My mom is very special to me because she loves me the way I am. My mom is also very loving because she is always there for me. Even if I do something wrong, she will always love me. She is also very caring because when I am sick, she is there for me. She is also caring because when she works, she has a smile on her face and a good humour about what is going on. Now that is why I love my mom.

I can always look up to her about stuff. When I have questions, she tells me the answers. She always helps me with my homework and teaches me the stuff I need to know like math.

My mom is thankful for everything she has, especially me and my sister. She's happy even when she is sick. I love you and never forget it!

By Angelina Cardelli, 11

Pam Ouellette

My mom is funny, nice and helpful. She teaches me about the word of God. Here is a little short story about God:

One night, I was reading my bible when my mom came in and said, 'do you want to know what I learned in church today?', so I said yes. She told me that God is going to come back and that we should be prepared. So I went over to my closet and got my suitcase and she started to laugh. After that, we said a prayer and I went to bed.

That is the end of my story. And one more thing: if it wasn't for my mom, I would not be here today. I love my mom.

By Casey Ouellette, 8

Josie Desrosiers

My mom is always helping other people. She helped my dad when he fell off the roof. She helped this little boy named Chase. He and his friends were playing grounder and he was going down the bar stairs on a jungle gym. He fell through the crack and had a tiny seizure.

My mom called 911 for help. She is a nurse, so she knows what to do. She spends a lot of time taking care of old people in nursing homes, as well as our family. Whenever someone is sick, she always knows what to do, like giving us medicine or ice packs.

My mom is a really good person. She always wants to help people, even when they're sick or injured. She takes them to get what they need, or takes them out to have some fun. My mom inspires me to do my best and to succeed. I have a dream to be just like my mom, but through helping animals. I would like to be a veterinarian.

Sometimes, my mom takes me to her work. We have fun. My favourite part was when she introduced me to a sick, 38-year-old girl named Darlene. She has Down's Syndrome and she loves to colour. So, I bring my colouring things and colour with her. My mom's work is cool. Her friends are cool too.

My mom's name is Josie. Mom is a hard worker and always makes sure we have what we need. I think my mom works too hard and too much. My family tries to give her a break once in a while. My mom and I enjoy shopping together, going for walks and listening to music. We watch our favorite shows together. We talk about a lot of things. She always tries to guide me into good paths. She always tells me to follow my heart, to try my best and to be kind to others. I love my mom so much. She is my best friend. My mom is the best mom in the world and I will never forget her. I want to be just like her.

by Nadia Desrosiers, 10

Bonnie

Bonnie is my hero because she takes care of me. Bonnie is my foster mom. I have lived with Bonnie for about three years. In these three years, Bonnie has taken me places and has been very good to me. Bonnie is a great hero to me and my brother, Mark, because she is so caring.

By Patrick, 8

Tracy Michauville

My mom is my hero because she catches me when I slide!

By Kaya Michauville, 5

Rosie Winterburn

My hero is my mom because she does everything for me. She buys me clothes and all of that stuff. If I do not like them, I just say they are cool. The best thing is that I love her and she loves me. She is the best thing that ever happened to me. I will not love anybody the way I love her. I will love her forever and ever. She even put me in hockey because I like it. It is really fun because if I am not doing a good job, she will cheer me on anyway. We have a good time together.

By Madison Winterburn, 9

Aimee Osas

My hero is my mom because she is loving and caring. She was born in Medicine Hat, Alberta, in 1977. She takes very good care of me and my sisters. She loves us with all her heart. I love my mom because she's very nice. I love my mom!

By Brady Benoit, 9

Keri Schierl

My hero is my mom because she does a lot of things. She takes care of us. She does the dishes, the laundry and helps us clean the living room. She cooks dinner and helps us clean our rooms. She lets us paint the pictures we want to paint.

When I am a teenager she is going to change my life by getting me driver's lessons and teaching me how to cook. I want to be a chef and my mom has tons of recipes.

By Mason Schierl, 6

nofrills™
lower food prices

MIKE AND LORI'S NO FRILLS
975 McKeown Ave., North Bay ON   495-4884
JEFF and TANIS' NO FRILLS
300 Lakeshore Dr., North Bay ON   494-9038

New Horizons Hair Team has been our business on Cassells Street for 8 years. We are very proud of our new renovations.

The relaxing and positive atmosphere is a real treat. We have four stylists:

- Donna Lynn
- Celine
- Debbie
- Melissa

All our stylists take classes and seminars annually to improve and stay updated on new and exciting styles.

Hours
Monday - closed
Tuesday - 8:30 - 5:30
Wednesday - 9:00 - 8:00
Thursday - 9:00 - 8:00
Friday - 8:30 - 5:30
Saturday - 8:30 - 3:00
Sunday - closed

Appointment not always necessary

Call us or contact us on our website to schedule an appointment - www.hairteam.ca

705·476·5148

673 Cassells Street, North Bay, Ontario P1B 4A1
www.hairteam.ca · e-mail: newhorizons@hairteam.ca

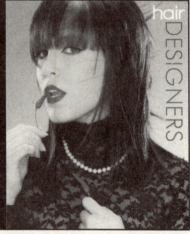

the Hair Designers

211 Main St. E., North Bay
705-472-8069

VIDA SALON

103 Worthington St. W., North Bay, ON
705-476-1444

WHIZ KIDZ
Consignment Store

GEAR FURNITURE AND CLOTHING FOR YOUR CHILD

www.whizkidz.ca

174 Oak Street West, North Bay, Ontario

705-223-WHIZ (9449)

kids
HOME ACCENTS

179 Main St. W.
North Bay, ON
705-494-8435

Yukon Bunk Bed

Yukon Crib

INFANT FURNITURE, PRODUCTS AND EVERYTHING TO DECORATE YOUR CHILD'S ROOM.

BEDDING, WALL DECOS AND MORE!

JUNIOR WORLD
children's clothing & footwear

High quality children's clothing, accessories and footwear for girls and boys sizes newborn to 14 years

Photo by Photo Metro

193 Main St. W., North Bay, - 476-5141

The Local Experts™

Jean Jamieson **Trevor Thomas**
Broker Sales Representative

www.gotyourbackrealty.com

Century21 Blue Sky Region Realty Inc. Brokerage
199 Main Street East   North Bay, ON P1B 2A5

Phone: **705-474-4500**
Email: jjamieson@c21northbay.com
Email: tthomas@century21northbay.com

CHAPTER SIX

OUR COMMUNITY

...A community needs a soul if it is to become a true home for human beings. You, the people, must get it this soul.

Pope John Paul II

North Bay Fire Fighters

The fire fighters from North Bay are my heroes for lots of reasons. They include putting on the haunted house at Halloween, teaching kids about fire safety and letting schools visit the fire department.

My most important reasons started on a snowy, Thursday night. There was a fire on Douglas St. My stepdad, Jamie, was going to the store and he ran back inside and said to my mom, "your sister's apartments are on fire." My mom jumped up and ran outside. When my mom came back in later that night, she told me everything that had happened. When she got outside, my mom and some other people called 911 to let the fire department know there was a fire. The fire fighters came very fast. They did their very best to put it out and to make sure that it didn't start any more fires in the buildings that were close to it.

When the fire was put out, they found that Deb was still in her apartment and she had passed away. My mom brought Deb's dog, Sammy, to our house so we could take care of him. The firemen had to go into the building and let some other animals out of their apartments. When the firemen had made sure that everything was safe, the people on the second and third floors could go into their homes.

The fire fighters are my heroes because they saved Aunt Cindy's apartment building and they tried their best to save Deb. They are very brave because they have an important and dangerous job that keeps us safe from fire. My mom says that people don't say thank you enough to the fire fighters and I think she is right so . . . thank you North Bay Fire Department.

By Emma Lodge, 8

Dave Tralevan
(My Friendly Neighbour)

My neighbour, Dave, was born with a disability (Down's Syndrome). This was very bad because they have a shortened life expectancy. Dave lived until he was over 50. Dave could barely walk down the stairs without falling. One night, Dave fell down the stairs and his mom called us for help. I really wanted to help but my parents said I was too young. It was a windy and stormy night outside. I was sitting on the outside step, waiting to see if Dave was alright. Then my parents came out and said he was fine. Soon after, he was sent to the hospital. A few days later, he died.

Dave has inspired me because no matter how many times he fell down, he just got right back up and continued with his life. He knew a lot of people and I'm almost positive that they all were inspired by Dave in different ways. He was special to me for who he was!

By Jacob Dubeau, 11

Dr. Pokrant

As soon as I was born, I was purple because the umbilical cord was wrapped around my neck and I couldn't breathe. Dr. Pokrant took me right away, unwrapped the umbilical cord from around my neck and put me under a heat lamp. After that, I was just a little, pink baby again!

By Selena Schaefer, 9

Antoinette McParland

My piano teacher, Antoinette, is one of my heroes because she helps me learn new songs. I like the songs that she teaches me. She teaches me piano so that I can get better and better. I really like playing the piano. I like how she helps me when I play the wrong note. I go to piano every Tuesday. I get very excited for my lesson. I got a keyboard for Christmas and I practice my songs every night to improve. Antoinette makes me feel good because she rewards me with stickers and so far I've received a sticker on every page.

By Sierra Neil, 7

North Bay Police Officers

The police officers are my heroes because they put the bad guys in jail so they don't do anything bad.

Sara Dufresne, 5

North Bay Fire Fighters

The fire fighters are my heroes because they save kitty cats.

By Riley Piché, 5

The Neighbours of Shields Point Road

It all happened when we got a phone call while we were camping. Our neighbour was on the phone saying that a tree crashed onto our house and told us to come home. We said we were happy there and that we didn't want to come home to a crashed house.

When we did go home, our house was fixed. There were just a few pieces of our banister that were broken. The tree was cut up on our lawn. Oh, were we happy when we got in the house. There were things scattered all over the floor, but all the work we would have had to do was done. Besides the clean up and the banister, we were so happy because our neighbours had done it all. They were our heroes and we thank them a lot.

By Janet Shaw, 10

Dr Carter

Bonjour! Mon nom est Alex et mon héros est Dr Carter parce que je suis allé lui voir trois fois et il m'a fait sentir très bien chaque fois.

Mon premier accident était quand j'avais 5 ans. Je suis allé faire du patinage sur ma patinoire sans casquette. Qu'est-ce que tu penses est arrivé? .....BOOM! Ahhhoucchhh!! Oui, mon menton a cassé et Dr Carter m'a suturé en trente minutes. Je ne peux pas voir les points de suture maintenant.

Mon deuxième accident, j'avais des problèmes avec ma tête. Mon héros a discuté avec moi à propos d'une solution possible et après un an, il a trouvé une pilule pour ma tête. Merci, Dr. Carter.

Mon troisième accident est arrivé au hockey, lorsqu'une personne a frappé son bâton de hockey sur ma jambe. Elle n'était pas la même, donc je suis allé voir Dr Carter et il a trouvé que s'était prise dans une place anormale. Alors, il l'a travaillé pendant trois jours. Ensuite, il a pu la bouger encore.

Dr Carter a fait beaucoup de choses pour moi et il va faire beaucoup de choses pour moi dans le futur... mais on n'espère pas trop!

Par Alexander Hurley, 10

Do you know a women who has touched your life?

PLEASE TELL US ABOUT HER!

(SEE OTHER SIDE FOR MORE DETAILS)

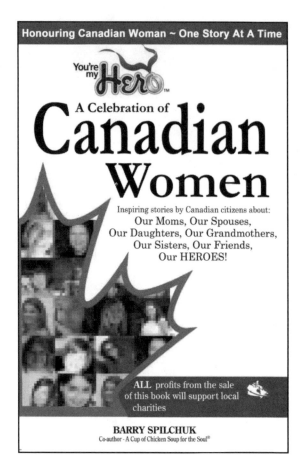

Please go to: **YMHbooks.com**
Click on: **Submit a story for the first time**
Click on: **CANADIAN WOMEN**
And input your story.

Both of your names will appear in our new book!

Shelley Dubeau
(Helping the Challenged)

When I first met Shelly Dubeau, I was inspired because she told me that she helped mentally challenged people. She helps kids that have abusive parents. That has inspired me because it would take a lot of patience to help mentally challenged people every day. She has been working for child and family services for 20 years. Shelly Dubeau must have helped a lot of people. She is so dedicated. It must take awhile to comfort all the people over the years.

Ever since I met her, I've wanted to help a challenged person. I don't know if I could help challenged people every day, but I would try because I know helping people is the right thing to do.

By Curtis Hebert, 11

Emergency Medical Services (EMS)

The people of the Emergency Medical Services (police, ambulance and fire) are my heroes. I haven't had to call 911 yet, but I may have to one day and I know that if I am ever in trouble I can count on them to help!

I just recently took the baby-sitting course and was taught all about safety. If I call 911, they will come to my rescue. These people work day and night to keep us safe. We should be very thankful! They stay at their station and wait for somebody to be in need. Sometimes they don't even get a call but they are always ready. Think about their family. They probably never see the rescue worker. Did you know that the rescue workers have to work on holidays including Christmas, Easter, Family Day and many more? I think that others should think more about their families. These rescue workers risk their lives for us and some are even volunteers! They are pretty special people.

A good example of a time that they saved us was on Highway 400. It was about a year ago. We were travelling back from my cousin's house in Stratford. There was a major crash. A transport truck was forced off the highway because of three cars racing. We were there for over 4 hours but it would have been longer if it wasn't for the emergency medical services. While we were waiting, another car waiting blew up under a bridge just meters away from our car. Just minutes later, the fire was out thanks to the fire fighters! That is just one example of when EMS came to the rescue! So think more about what they are doing for us next time you hear a siren.

By Nicholas Waltenbury, 10

Ambulance Attendant
(Come Quick!)

One night, I was watching TV on the stairs. When I got up, a sharp part of the stairs went right into my head. My dad came down to see if I was alright and he picked me up. That's when he felt the blood dripping down his arm.

So he rushed me to the bathroom. My mom came in and she said, "What is going on?" My dad told her what had happened and my mom put me in the sink and told my dad to get a wet towel. He came back with my mom's only white towel. There was so much blood on it, it almost filled it. Then my dad asked my mom if he should call 911. The ambulance came very quickly. The ambulance attendant came in and asked what happened. They looked at my head and asked me questions. They told my mom that I was going to be fine and that I didn't have to have stitches. I was so happy. That is why the ambulance attendant is my hero.

By Ryan Vendetti, 7

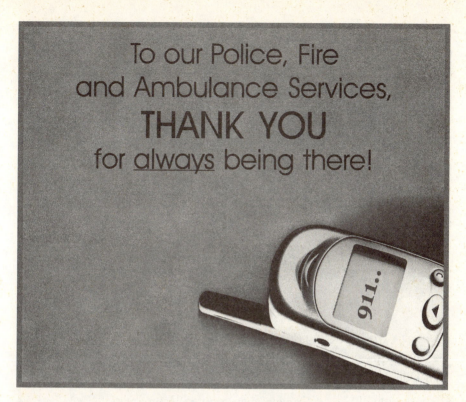

INN ON THE BAY
HOTEL · RESTO CAFÉ · MEETINGS

main street unique

Whether you're visiting for a day or an extended period of time, our Inn is the premier place for comfortable accommodations and fine dining. Including...

- Conveniently Located Downtown
- Jacuzzi and Fireplace Suites
- 100% Smoke Free
- Wireless Internet Access
- Resto Café Room Service
- Private Meeting Room
- Off-site Catering
- Resto Café (Open Weekdays & Weekends)

www.innonthebay.ca
340 Main Street East • North Bay ON • P1B 9V1
For Reservations call 1.877.937.8483

1325 Seymour Street
North Bay, ON
P1B 9V6
Phone: (705) 476-7700
Fax: (705) 476-7760

www.hiexpress.com/northbayon

Wherever life takes you
in North Bay...
Best Western is there.

THE WORLD'S LARGEST HOTEL CHAIN

You'll always be home
when you stay at
Best Western North Bay!

Best Western North Bay

700 Lakeshore Drive, North Bay, Ontario P1A 1G4
705-474-5800
1-800-461-6199   BestWesternNorthBay.com

CONGRATULATIONS

to the staff at
CALLANDER BAY DENTAL CENTRE
for raising over

$211,080.00

through their participation in

ALI   ANNIKA   DEB   JESSICA   KAREN   KELLY   LAURIE   LINDY

MARYLOU   MELISSA   MICHELLE   SALLY   SHARON   SHARON   SHEILA   SUZANNE

DR. MARIO   DR. LARRY

299 Main Street North, Callander ON   705-752-1510

CHAPTER SEVEN

OUR GRANDMOTHERS

We should all have one person who knows how to bless us despite the evidence, Grandmother was that person to me.

Phyllis Theroux

Simone Skuro

She was the most important person in the world to me. Through the rough times and the easy times, she was always standing there holding my hand. She was my grandma.

Grandma was always there to yell at my aunt because she was telling me silly stories, or to warn my grandpa that I was about to come zipping around the corner and jump in his lap. I remember always using my army of squirty toys to spray her from head to toe. Now these were only some of the good times! We had even bigger amounts of fun running bare-bum down the hallway (I was only three) and kicking my ball around the house. I really wish she was still here.

One day, the horrible news came. My grandma was very sick in the hospital and she had a problem with her lungs. I wasn't very worried because my grandma taught me to be a 'tough cookie' and that all bad things turn out to be okay. But this was different. Of course, I was too young to understand what was going on but I knew this was bad. She died that day. My mom and I were wrecks.

My grandma taught me that life is like a roller coaster and that ups and downs are always coming your way. I really miss her hugs and love taps, but I'll always remember the great times we had together and what she taught me.

By Julia Allard, 10

Linda Teeple

When I was a baby, my grandma made me clothes that fit because when I was a baby, nothing fit! It was all too big. It started when I was born. My mom couldn't find anything to fit except doll clothes. Gramma offered to make clothes for me. So today, my grandma makes all my clothes, my doll clothes and knits me sweaters. For my birthday, my grandma got me a sewing kit so she can teach me how to sew. Then, I can make stuff for myself.

By Kayleigh Durocher, 9

Vita Young

Gokmis is the Anishinabe word for grandmother. When my Gokmis was a little girl her dad was a fisherman. He went out in a boat for six months to a year. When he was away, his wife died. My Gokmis was seven years old and she had two younger brothers, Pat and Mat. When her mom died, the whole village came to bury Gokmis's mom.

Gokmis, Pat, and Mat could no longer live in the house where their mother died, leaving them orphaned. Times were very poor and no one could help them. So they had to go from house to house asking for food and to live in other people's homes. They usually had to live in a shed or the barn. Sometimes when there was no place for them, they slept in ditches.

They had to work hard for food. They often got beaten up if they did something wrong or if the people they lived with were drunk or mean. When Mat and Pat were old enough, they joined the army and went away to war. When Gokmis was old enough, she went to Toronto to get a job and met my misomis, Goppy. This is why my Gokmis is my hero. If she hadn't survived that, she would have died and I wouldn't be alive. I love my Gokmis.

By Wylden Ray, 9

Claire Foisy

Grandma was my best friend. She gave me a roof over my head with my mom and dad. She always played with me and made me happy when I was sad. I could tell you lots of stories, but the one that I remember most was this:

It was a warm summer day and me and my grandma were sitting out in the yard. The birds were singing and the sun was shining. We were eating cheese and crackers. It was yummy! My grandma went to go change into cooler clothes. She asked me to take the hose and clean the chairs we were sitting on. They were full of crumbs. So, I took the hose and instead of washing the chairs, I sprayed her! She stood like a statue for a moment and then yelled, "Serena. I'm all soaked!" I laughed and she started to, too. Then she went in. When she came out, she was in new clothes and I washed the chairs. We had so much fun the rest of the day.

What is disappointing was she passed away last year. I was so sad. I used to tell her all my secrets. I want her back on ground just once. I want to talk to her again. If I go in my school yard and look by this one tree, I think I can see her face. I made a grave on the ground with sticks and rocks. I believe she watches over me and I believe she helps me out when I need it. I loved her a lot. She will always be in my heart. I'll always remember her as my angel.

By Serena Foisy, 10

Carmaine McQuabbie

My grandmother is my hero because she helped me get out of foster care. When I was in foster care, we didn't go to school. If I was still in foster care, I wouldn't have friends because I didn't go to school. I live with my grandmother. When I am sick, she takes care of me. She helps me with my homework. She makes sure that I have good food and a nice house to live in. She let me keep my cat. She lets me feed stray cats that don't have food to eat.

By Marlanda McQuabbie, 8

Lise Bellaue

When I was very little, my grandmother used to sit down with me and read the same book over and over again. When we were done I would ask her to read the book again and she would read it again until I fell asleep.

My grandma is very kind. When we go to visit her, she makes a batch of her famous caramels. Just thinking about it makes me want to go to her house right now! Whenever I am around her, she makes me feel special in every way. I love my grandma!

My grandma never forgets my birthday and she'll drive 500 kilometres to support me in special events. She will also call us from time to time to see how we're doing. Sometimes we call her to see how she's doing and she always wants to talk to me.

By Kiara Brouillette, 11

Linda Mathias
(A Bear Island Hero)

My grandma, Linda Mathias, is wonderful and a great role model. My grandma Linda has supported me through all my endeavours and continues to support me. She has been my hero ever since I was able to say 'mama'.

Grandma Linda was born on March 1st, 1947, in Haileybury, Ontario. Grandma is the only girl of six children. Growing up with five brothers was not easy. She always wished for a sister. She did not get her sister but she has three granddaughters. She is so proud and extremely happy to have granddaughters.

Grandma has lived in Haileybury, North Bay and Bear Island. She returned to her Ojibwa community, Bear Island, when her children were young. She realized that she wanted to raise her children on Bear Island so they could understand the Ojibwa culture and language.

There are many good qualities that my grandmother possesses. First, she is outgoing, caring, loving, honest, fun and adventurous. Without these characteristics my grandma would be a different grandma. Everyone should have a fun spirit inside them like her.

Second, she is a loving grandma who truly loves me and my sisters, but also our hockey teams. She gets right into the sport and is very supportive at games and tournaments.

Third, she cares for us through all circumstances. When my foot hurts or I have a cut on my foot or my knee hurts, she always helps me. If I need a shoulder to lean on or I just need a big hug, she is always there with open arms, a big heart and a helping hand.

Without her my life would be incomplete; it would be like half of my heart was missing. I love Grandma Linda. You should take the time to meet this incredible woman with such an amazing personality.

By: Demi Mathias

Sharon Larmand

My grandma and I are best friends. We love to write books. Our first book was 'The Musical Bear'. My grandma has cancer; but I still love my grandma. She is very healthy now. She takes a lot of pills. She'll go shopping with me and my mom. She'll go do groceries with me and my mom. She loves playing with me and Mason. My grandma and I both love each other a lot. The way my grandma inspires me is in how she teaches me. She teaches me how to read, spell and writes stories. If she was a teacher, she would be the best teacher.

By Emma Lee Burgess, 8

Shirley Duchesne

My nanny has taken me for lots of girl days. My nanny's name is Shirley Duchesne and she was in the original book. My nanny helped lots of people just like me. I never got to say goodbye. My nanny did lots for me. I always slept over. We went to the mall and the movies, but the best time of the day would always be bedtime . . . and the bed is so warm and cozy. My nanny was loved by all. She's an angel, I just know it. I loved her lots. She was so caring. Lots of people felt very sad when she left. She was the best. I know that.

By Gabrielle Duchesne, 9

Frances Lees
(The Gift of my Hero)

Every summer I would go to my cottage in Winnipeg to see my great-grandparents. When I was seven, my great-grandma became very ill. A week before my birthday, she died. A couple of days afterwards, I got a parcel in the mail for my birthday. It was from my great-grandma. It was a designer pillow, a diary and a pen. So she is my hero because she thought of me and gave me a gift even though she was very sick and not very wealthy.

By Mackenzie Gregson, 9

Gina Cicciarelli

My nonna was born in Italy, in a little place called Naples. She immigrated to Canada when she was only 9 years old, which made it hard for her in school because she had to learn a whole new language.

Nonna is like most grandmas, but there are a few different things about her that make her who she is. Whenever I go to her house, no matter what has happened throughout the day, she is always in a good mood. It's like she forgets about everything around her and is just happy to see us.

Nonna is always there for me no matter where I am or what I did. When you need someone there beside you, she will be there. If you need something from her right that minute, she will just drop everything that she's doing and come. When I think about this right now, I find it just amazing.

Nonna is the kind of person who will never give up on me or anyone else. Even if I start to give up, she won't because she knows that I can do it. When she does this, it makes me feel good.

Nonna has been through some rough patches in her life but she has stayed strong and kept moving on. That is one characteristic that I like about her because when things are going bad I know that she will make them right.

By Amanda White, 12

Talk to us first for your financial needs.

3 North Bay locations to serve you . . .

240 Main St. E.	North Bay Mall	2031 Cassells St.
(705) 472-4370	300 Lakeshore Dr.	(705) 474-3421
	(705) 474-1724	

 Canada Trust

Banking can be this comfortable

THE CHINA CABINET
Tableware & Gifts

177 Main Street West
North Bay, ON P1B 2T6

www.chinacabinetonline.com

(705) 474-8619
1-866-302-7467

Greco's Pizza of North Bay Ontario creates your favorite oven roasted pizza. In 1913, Oscar Greco founded Greco's Bakery, adopting as his motto "The Taste Will Tell." Oscar's son Cecil, born that same year, and raised in the bakery developed a natural talent and love for baking. He opened the original Greco's Pizza in 1969, retaining the quality and pride in service learned at his father's side.

EAT-IN * TAKE-OUT * DELIVERY

344 Algonquin Ave.
705-474-6322

221 Lakeshore Dr.
705-476-4111

CHAPTER EIGHT

OUR GRANDFATHERS

What children need most are the essentials that grandparents provide in abundance. They give unconditional love, kindness, patience, humor, comfort, lessons in life. And, most importantly, cookies.

Rudolph Giuliani

Keats Williamson

I'm writing about my great-great-grandfather who was in World War II. He saved lots of people's lives. His name was Keats, like my cousin and me. I wanted to meet him. I want to know so much.

This is how he saved so many lives during the war. He rode around on a motorcycle and cut the barbed wire so that the people in the cars wouldn't have their heads cut off. After the war, he survived and went back to his family. He died of cancer 20 years later. Then, his name got passed down to me. I have the same name as my great-great-grandfather, Keats, a name I'm proud to share.

by Keats Vanderlee, 9

Bob Pincivero

My grandpa, Bob Pincivero, was born in Pisterzo, Italy. He is probably one of the most fun grandpas in the world. He's the most fun because he is athletic, enjoyable, funny and really good at games.

He's a grandpa and he still plays golf and curls. He's fantastic at it. He even got a hole-in-one at Highview Golf Course (hole 10). Sometimes I golf with him and he slaughters me. He curls in the winter almost every day. I am terrible at curling so if I played with him he'd destroy me.

My grandpa is so enjoyable because he's really funny and he does the most incredible things with you. I used to go to his house every day before school, when I was in SK. The funny part about my grandpa is when people get older they get grumpier, but my grandpa is "degrumpifiyng" (he's getting less grouchy).

My grandpa plays cards, Yahtzee and Triominos with me. His favourite game of cards is Crazy Eights and 7up. He's not very lucky because I almost always beat him at Yahtzee and Triominos. Sometimes I watch T.V. with him and other times I help him peel potatoes or make gnocchi. I admire my grandpa because he's a grandpa and he'll play sports. I'm glad he's Italian because I love helping him make gnocchi. He's the most magnificent grandpa in the world and I wouldn't exchange him for anything, not even Bill Gates.

By Steven Sherry, 10

Dave Decost
(Average, Ordinary, Everyday Superhero)

Ever since I can remember, my pappy, Dave Decost, has always been there for me. He's come to every one of my birthdays and when I need someone to talk to, he's there beside me. He is my sidekick, my partner in crime. Even though he's my grandfather, with everything he does for me, he may as well be my dad.•

As I think back, my pappy has done a lot. When I was four years old, he took me fishing. Some people ask what the big deal is about fishing. I never said it was a big deal, it just meant the world to me. It was really windy that day and the waves were insanely high. I remember catching a really big pike. When we brought it into the net, I screamed. It snapped the line on my purple fishing rod and got away. When my pappy and I went to a different fishing spot, the wind blew us into a rock bed. He was leaning over the side of the boat and he nearly fell in the lake. He let me drive the boat for my very first time and we sang "The Yellow Submarine" together. I learned on that fishing trip that fish in the lake are way bigger than the ones in the fish tank. When I was 13, my pappy decided to teach me how to actually start and drive a boat. At first, I was scared but when I saw my cousin doing it, I knew I could. It was amazing. I was going fast enough for my liking and then my pappy told me to open it right up. I didn't know what he meant and I gave him a 'hello-I-don't-understand-fishermen-lingo'. He explained that it meant to make the boat go its fastest. I drove it to Callander and back to North Bay.

During the winter of 1999, I learned how to operate a backhoe. The company my pappy works for can't put up fences during the winter so some of them clear parking lots. He let me drive the backhoe from Acme Welding to his house on Worthington. Lucky for us, a police officer was behind us and no one got into any trouble. During the same winter, we were clearing the parking lot at the Super 8 Motel. On our way home, we went to Dairy Queen. That was the first time I tried a banana split. Every once in awhile, he reminds me what I said to him when I was eating it, "It's so good. I just can't help myself."

When I was younger, I used to go to my grandparent's house on Friday nights after school. On Saturday mornings my pappy and I would go for rides in the country. I still go with him sometimes, but now we're usually busy doing other things. He makes lunches on Sunday and I go on the weekend that I'm not at my dad's house.

My pappy didn't perform a miracle to be a hero, he just had to be a part of my life and for that I'm truly happy. I'm glad I had the chance to experience the fun things with my grandpa that other kids might not get to experience with their grandparents. He has his downfalls, just like me, but I'm proud to say that he's my best friend!

By Kyleigh Decost, 13

Diego Udeschini

My nonno was born on May 4th in Italy. His real name is Diego Udeschini and I admire him because he is a very tough old bird and he is always there for me. Have you ever heard of Popeye? My nonno is very much like Popeye. He has big muscles. His muscles are so huge that when he flexes, they are hard like a rock.; well actually, a boulder.

My nonno worked in a mine in Elliot Lake. I think that working there has really toughened him up. My nonno also worked as an electrician and he got shocked by an electrical pole. He says it's no big deal when he hurts himself. Whenever I am home alone, he invites me over to his house. When I am working on my math homework, he helps with questions. He also wants to play cards with me like Golf, Crazy Eights, Go Fish and pretty much every card game. He has also taught me a lot of life skills.

All my life, my nonno has been there for me. He is the greatest nonno because he has taught me everything I know about electricity, wood working and life skills. I love my nonno so much and the good thing is, he lives right around the block so I can see him often.

By Max Udeschini, 11

John McGrinder

When my papa was younger, he was a policeman. I know he misses that job because I hear him telling my dad about catching the bad guys. This April, my papa will get a special award from the police called Top Cop. It's a secret. He doesn't know about it.

Since he retired, he took on a new job as Santa Claus. The children all love him as much as he loves putting on that red suit. He goes to different schools and homes at Christmas time, along with Mrs. Claus (my mama), to bring joy to the little ones.

Five years ago, my papa got cancer. His only worry about the disease was about feeling well for Christmas. My papa was okay for awhile, but now the cancer is back. We all pray that papa will beat this again and have many more Christmases to come.

He is honest, caring and good. He does a lot for his town. They even gave him the award for Citizen of the Year. I hope that when I grow up, I can marry a man as good as my papa.

By Emilly Chenier, 11

Stefano D'Agostino
(The Last Time I Saw You)

Nonno, the last time I saw you, you were lying on a hospital bed and I whispered, "Nonno, can you be my guardian angel?"

I thought of all the good times we had together, like when we would go on walks and talk about nature and your garden. We would race to see who could eat the most dinner; but, most of all, I can't forget my nonno taught me that family always comes first.

Nonno, I know that I can always look up to you even if you're not with me anymore. You can talk to me in my prayers, my dreams and your love. Nonno, I know you're still with me each and every day and there's not a day that passes that we don't think about you and the sparkle in your eye. I'll never forget you, Nonno.

By Elaine D'Agostino, 9

Leo Rainer

My opa, Leo Rainer, has never said 'no' to anything for as long as I've known him. The time that blows me out of the water is when he said 'yes' to fight in World War II. If he didn't, he would get killed and his family would too. Amazingly, his strength held him together and he survived the war. Now in his old age, he still does dangerous things. He had asked my dad to let him help build our sleep cabin, which had a thirty foot drop off the edge.

My opa had a rough past. His mom died when he was just a little boy and he had the worst of stepmothers and sisters. They treated him like a speck of dirt! Along with his terrible past, he had to join the Nazi invasion at just 18 years old. Later on in his life, he also had his wife pass away from a horrible disease.

My opa is the toughest man you'd ever meet. When going through the toughest of times, he never lost faith. He has overcome many obstacles and today he is here for his family.

By Jackson Newman, 12

John Thayer

My grandpa is 60 years old and was born in a small town in Quebec. He lives in Ontario and owns his own company. My grandpa's goals in life are to live a long and happy life with his wife, children and grandchildren. He has been married for 40 years.

My grandpa is my hero because about one year ago, he found out that he had cancer. Since then, he has had radiation therapy 42 times and it did not work. He ended up having a big operation to take out his voice box out. He has a hole in his neck that he breathes out of called a stoma. This sounds really bad but his cancer is gone, so we think it is good. In December, he got something in his throat that lets him talk when he covers his hole. He is happy he can talk again.

I learned from my grandpa that if you have a positive attitude, you can do anything. I learned how important family is. He also taught me that just because you have no voice, it does not mean you can't accomplish things. Even though he couldn't talk, he still worked, went to the grocery store and many other places. He just had to write when he wanted to talk to people. I like to do many things with my grandpa. We hunt, fish and camp. He also taught me how to play poker.

A good thing about my grandpa is that he lives next door, so I can see him whenever I want. He helps me fix my ski-doo and my four-wheeler whenever it breaks down. When I grow up, I want to be just like my grandpa. He is funny, loving, courageous and selfless. He is courageous because even though he has a disability, he still smiles. That's something that I will never forget.

By Mason Birmingham, 11

Steve Molnar

My Hero is my Grandfather whom I call my Poppa. He is my Hero because he has done so much for me and still does.

When I was very young, my poppa would baby-sit me. We use to do so many things together. We use to play games, my favourite was playing cards. We would watch TV everyday, over and over and over, Land Before Time and Barney and Hi-5. You would think he would get tired of it but he never did. He was always so kind to me, he would just smile every time I would ask him to watch them over and over again. That's when I knew he loved me.

Poppa always took me for walks, and out to special places to eat. Places like McDonalds and of course my all time favourite place and where he still takes me today is Burger World.

My Poppa always listens to me when I need someone to talk to and he loves me no matter what.

My Poppa treats me to anything I want and I would do the same for him.

To me, my poppa is the best poppa ever and I hope someday I can make him proud of me. He means the whole wide world to me.

I love you Poppa and thank you. You are the best.

By Amanda Molnar, 9

Bob Lawryniw

My great-grandfather was born in the Ukraine in 1922. He overcame a lot of hardships such as the famine in 1932 in which eight million people died. When this occurred, he didn't have food for three days.

In 1939, he was involved in the war and was a prisoner of war. He escaped with two other men. My great-grandfather travelled through Romania, Croatia, Hungary, Solvakia, Italy, Germany, Austria and the U.S.A.

It took ten days by boat to come to Canada. In 1948, he applied for a job at the Paymaster Mine in Timmins, Ontario. He worked in the mines underground for 25 years until he got hurt.

My great-grandfather then opened a convenience store where he also sold coins. He can't see very well now but continues to sell coins. He has started me on my own coin collection. I enjoy hearing all his stories.

At 85 years old, he has got a sense of humour and is always willing to help others in need. I admire this great man for all he has done for me and my family. HE IS MY HERO!!!

By Adam Cucullo, 10

Alfred Morin
(A Brave Heart)

My great-grandfather, who now lives at a retirement home in Sudbury with his wife, was in World War II. When I was a little girl of 8 or 9, I sat and asked about the things he saw, the things he heard and the way he felt. He was never afraid to speak his mind. I'm sure it was hard to explain to a little girl.

The reason I feel this way is because he fought for me, you, your neighbours, your friends and your families, and tried very hard to keep us safe. I can only imagine how proud most of the soldiers were when Germany surrendered. My great-grandfather was part of that success story.

Coming back to Sudbury with half a finger was the least of his worries. Being one of the few survivors, I believe, would be a proud day. I think the most upsetting part of this historical event was watching a couple of his good friends pass away. Some were the bravest people he'd ever met.

He has many character traits that I imagine other people don't have. He has the courage to move forth, even though he's seen thousands die. When you're scared, you still go on.

My great-grandfather is truly an inspiration to me and even though I don't visit him much anymore, I still remember many of the stories he has told me and I will remember them for as long as I live.

By Rebecca Olivier, 13

Vic Pettella

My nonno, Vic, is my hero. He is an old man. He helps people by fixing shoes. He is a good man. He sat on the couch to rest his hand and leg when he got hurt. He plays games with me and helps me.

By Michael Pettella, 6

TWO NORTH BAY LOCATIONS:

231 Lakeshore Dr.
and
Northgate Shopping Centre at
1500 Fisher St.

Custom Made Jewellery & Fine Repairs
Competitive Prices on Diamonds, Gems & Quality Coloured Stones

Peter Walsh, Original Owner for 42 Years in Goldsmithing

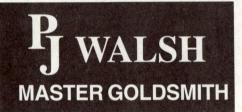

THE BEST SERVICE IN NORTHERN ONTARIO

pjandmj@efni.com
1720 Algonquin Ave, North Bay, ON
705-494-9948

Northern Comfort *Studio*
TANNING SALON & DAY SPA
• 5 Tanning Rooms • Nails
• Full Spa Services • Hair Design

320 Airport Rd. 705-474-4333

Scotiabank

NORTH BAY BUSINESS BANKING CENTRE
204 Main Street West
(705)494-4717

NORTHGATE SQUARE
1500 Fisher Street
(705)472-5680

NIPISSING PLAZA
390 Lakeshore Drive
(705)474-0140

YOU'RE RICHER THAN YOU THINK!

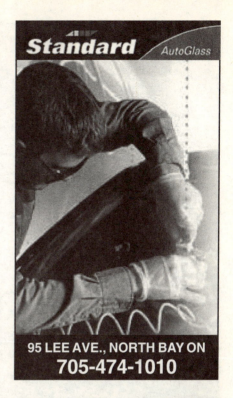

95 LEE AVE., NORTH BAY ON
705-474-1010

ProNorth Transportation

348 Birch's Road
North Bay, Ontario
(705) 476-4411

JUST LUBES
Oil Change Centres

RUSTBLOCK,
RUST PROOFING
& FULL AUTO
DETAILING
SERVICES

100 Golf Club Rd.
North Bay, ON P1B 8X7
(705) 494-7676

QUAKER STATE

CHAPTER NINE

OUR HEROES IN PICTURES

'What is the use of a book', thought Alice,
'without pictures or conversations?'

Lewis Carroll
from Alice in Wonderland

My brother is my hero because he helps me playing games.
By Alex Baker

God is my hero because He blesses me.
By Amy Oullette

My mommy is my hero because she takes care of me when I'm sick.
By Amaya Sorensen-Trudeau

My Mom and Dad are my heroes because they take care of me and bring me to the hospital when I am sick.
By Austin Cayen

OUR HEROES IN PICTURES

Police Officers

The police are my heroes because they saved me from a fire in my house.
By Bianca Beaucage

Cherie Penase

My Mom is my hero because she tucks me in at bedtime.
By Brock Penasse

My Grandpa

My grandpa is my hero because he takes care of me when I am sick.
By Brooke Malette

My Mommy

My hero is my mom because she tucked me in bed when I was a baby and she had a soft changing pillow.
By Brooklyn Thompson

OUR HEROES IN PICTURES

My Mom & Dad

My mom and dad are my heroes because they are special.
By Chase Penasse-McLeod

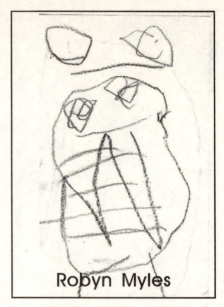

Robyn Myles

My mom, because she is good to me.
By Christopher Myles

Mme. Levac

Mme. Levac is my hero because she takes care of me at school.
By Cole Audet

My Dad

My dad is my hero because he plays with me.
By Darrien Philion

My dog Chief is my hero because he barks to tell us there is a bear.
By Deanna Harvey

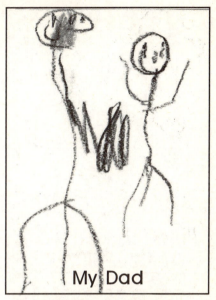

My dad - because he helps me get dressed.
By Devin Beaucage

My mom is my hero because she takes care of me.
By Drake Commanda

My mom and dad are my heroes because they take care of me when I am sick.
By Emilie Dagg

My Mom, Samantha

My mom is my hero because she takes care of me. My dad is my hero because he protects me.
By Emily Laforge

My Mom & Dad

My mom and dad are my heroes because they take care of me.
By Ericka Brazeau

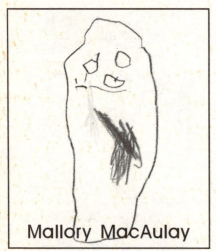

Mallory MacAulay

My sister Mallory is my hero because she lets me go in her room and sit on her bed to watch movies with her.
By Glen MacAulay

Michael & Geraldine

My Mom and dad are nice.
By Hailey Goulais

Take-out & Delivery Menu
www.grecospizza.ca

474-6322
344 Algonquin Ave.

Delivery to Most Areas
with minimum food orders.

...appetizers

GARLIC BREAD	$3.95
With mozzarella cheese	$4.95
With cheese and bacon	$5.95
CHEESE BREAD	$6.99
(with dipping sauce)	
FRIDAY BREAD	$6.95
(garlic butter, two types of cheese, back bacon and cajun spice)	
GRECO'S OWN BRUSCHETTA	$6.95
(garlic butter, two types of cheese, tomatoes and cajun spice)	

...subs & wraps° *whole wheat or regular*

°VEGGIE	$6.20	HALF $4.20
°ASSORTED	$6.20	HALF $4.20
HAM	$6.20	HALF $4.20
SALAMI	$6.20	HALF $4.20
CHEESE	$6.20	HALF $4.20
°B.L.T.	$7.20	HALF $4.75
SUPER	$8.95	HALF $6.20
PHILLY STEAK	$9.20	HALF 6.20
CLUB		$8.95
°TURKEY		$6.95
HOT CORNED BEEF		$6.95
BBQ CHICKEN		$7.20
HOT MEATBALL		$6.95
HOT ITALIAN SAUSAGE		$7.20

pitas *whole wheat or regular*

GREEK	$6.95
CAESAR	$6.95
VEGGIE	$6.95
CHEESE	$6.95
B.L.T.	$6.95
HAM	$6.95
TURKEY	$6.95
ASSORTED	$6.95
TUNA	$6.95
CLUB	$8.95
FAJITA	$12.95
Add chicken breast to any pita for only	$3.00

...mexican fiesta

FAJITAS (OR PITA)

Chicken or beef	$12.95
Stir fried mixed peppers & onions in olive oil with fresh garlic and cajun spice.	
Vegetable	$10.95
A blend of zucchini, mushrooms, tomatoes, mixed peppers & onions stir fried in olive oil with our fresh garlic and cajun spice.	
NACHOS	$7.95 HALF $5.95
NACHOS DELUXE	$11.95 HALF $9.95
Nacho's with tomatoes, mixed peppers, onions and extra cheese.	

BURRITO (WITH CHILI) OR ENCHILADA (WITHOUT CHILI)
Served with yellow rice and refried beans.

Beef steak or chicken	$12.95
Veggie (mushroom, black olive & broccoli)	$10.95
SEVEN LAYER DIP	$8.95
A layer of each: refried beans, guacamole, sour cream, tomatoes, black olives, onions & topped with nacho cheese. Served with nacho chips on the side. Try it hot or cold.	
QUESADILLAS	$7.95
3 flour tortillas stuffed with nacho cheese and baked. Served with sour cream & our fresh salsa	
Add Chicken	$3.50
Additional items	$1.25

Greco's Pizza & Pasta
344 Algonquin Ave.
North Bay ON
P1B 4W3
Tel: 474.6322
Fax: 474.2255
www.grecospizza.ca

July 2008

All prices from the menu do not include taxes & gratuities.

...Greco's specialty pizzas

VEGGIE
Pizza sauce, mozzarella, mushrooms, mixed peppers, black olives, onions & tomatoes.

GOURMET
Garlic butter, mozzarella, zucchini, cherry tomatoes, onions, cajun spice.

PESTO
Pesto sauce, tomatoes, onions, mushrooms, feta & a sprinkle of mozzarella.

MEXICAN
Pizza sauce, taco spice, nacho cheese, taco beef, onions topped with lettuce & fresh tomatoes. Jalapeno peppers are an option.

DELUXE
Pizza sauce, mozzarella, pepperoni, back bacon, ham, mushrooms, mixed peppers & black or green olives.

Sorry, no substitutions for toppings on Greco's specialty pizzas, only additions.

...pizza your way

	Mini-6"	Small-10"	Medium-12"	Large-14"	Family-16"
Cheese & Sauce	$6.25	$9.25	$12.50	$15.75	$18.50
1 Topping	$6.75	$10.00	$13.50	$17.00	$20.00
2 Toppings	$7.25	$10.75	$14.50	$18.25	$21.50
3 Toppings	$7.75	$11.50	$15.50	$19.50	$23.00
4 Toppings	$8.25	$12.25	$16.50	$20.75	$24.50
Additional Toppings	$0.50	$0.75	$1.00	$1.25	$1.50

Fresh Toppings

Pepperoni	Mushrooms	Mixed Peppers	Sun Dried Tomatoes
Back Bacon	Double Cheese	Tomatoes	Hot Banana Peppers
Black Olives	Green Olives	Salami	Meatballs
Onions	Italian Sausage	Anchovies	Jalapeno Peppers
Spinach	Zucchini	Broccoli	
		Taco Beef	
		Nacho Cheese	
		Feta (extra $1.00)	

Whole wheat or regular crust, thick or thin & extra sauce all at no extra cost!

...pasta your way

FULL ORDER................$10.95
HALF ORDER................$7.95

To start, choose your pasta:
Linguini, fettucini, spinach lettucini, penne, gluten free penne, tri-coloured fusili, tri-coloured spaghetti. Or choose the Cheese Tortellini for $3.00 more.

Next, choose your sauce:
Tomato, meat sauce, blush, pesto, garlic olive oil. Our fresh Alfredo sauce for $1.95 more.

For an extra $3.95, you can add:
2 meatballs, Italian sausage, chicken breast strips, sauteed mushrooms, sauteed mushrooms with peppers and onions or steamed carrots, cauliflower and broccoli.

Add 1 large meatball..................$2.25
Add an extra vegetable..............$1.25
Add feta cheese.........................$2.50
Add sauteed garlic shrimps........$4.95
Oven Baked with mozzarella......$2.25

LASAGNA................$11.25..HALF $9.95
Your choice of pasta, steamed carrots, cauliflower and broccoli served with our own Alfredo sauce.

PASTA PRIMAVERA..$15.95..HALF $9.95

GARIBALDI
CANNELONI............2 / $11.95..........1 / $8.95
Pasta rolls stuffed with Italian sausage, spinach & seasoning, topped with tomato sauce & mozzarella, and oven baked.

CHEESE
CANNELONI..............2 / $11.95.........1 / $8.95
Pasta rolls stuffed with Italian cheeses, garlic & seasoning, topped with tomato sauce, mozzarella and oven baked.

PENNE WITH GINGER
SHRIMP & PEPPERS......................$14.95
Shrimp, red, yellow and green peppers, and penne sauteed with fresh ginger and garlic in olive oil.

CAJUN PASTA............................$11.95
Tri-coloured spaghetti stir-fried in olive oil with zucchini, peppers, onions, fresh garlic & cajun spice.

...salads

Dress up your salad!!! Your choice of house, creamy cucumber, Italian, Italian light, French, sun dried tomato, blue cheese, 1000 islands, honey dijon, low fat ranch, buttermilk ranch, cusabi (creamy cucumber & wasabi), roasted red peppers & goat cheese, oil and vinegar or balsamic vinegar and olive oil. Try sunflower seeds on your salad!

CAESAR................$6.95
Our house specialty, romaine lettuce, tossed with our freshly made dressing, topped with croutons and real bacon bits.

CHEF................$6.50
Iceberg lettuce, radish, purple cabbage, carrot, tomato, cucumber & purple onions.

JULIENNE................$7.95
Chef salad with ham, salami, cheese & a pickled egg.

CHEDDAR BACON................$7.95
Our chef salad topped with back bacon & cheddar chunks.

GREEK................$7.95
Romaine lettuce blended with our chef salad & topped with Greek olives, feta and our own Greek dressing.

SPINACH................$7.95

SPINACH WITH
GOAT CHEESE................$9.95
Mushrooms, peppers and onions in olive oil and garlic on a bed of baby spinach topped with goat cheese. Try it with our roasted red pepper goat cheese dressing.

Add chicken breast strips to any salad for only................$3.00
sliced roasted turkey breast........$2.95
garlic shrimp..............................$4.95

OUR HEROES IN PICTURES

Stacey Fisher

My dad is my hero because if I
drown he will be there
to save me.
By Hayley Faith Fisher

**Me and Spiderman
are throwing paper.**

Spiderman is my hero because
the clouds come and he is
transforming the clouds
to do stuff.
By Jaydon Lachance

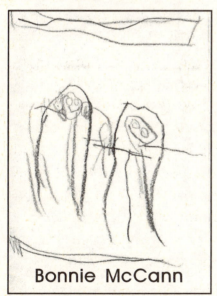

Bonnie McCann

My mom is my hero because she
lets me sleep in her room.
By Jennifer Dube

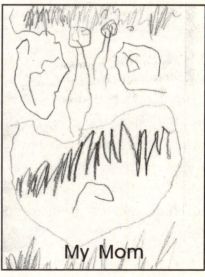

My Mom

My mom is my hero because she
takes care of me and sometimes
gives me chocolate.
By Jeremy Leavens

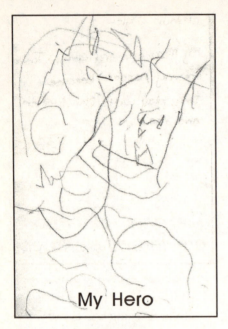

My Hero

I love my hero.
By Joshua Myles

Nurses

The nurses at the hospital are my hero because they take care of me.
By Kiera Becker

Uncle Cameron

My uncle Cameron is my hero because he kills animals for me to eat. My cousin Melcolm helps him.
By Kiley George

Sean Danis

My brother Sean is my hero because he always plays with me. My brother is my hero and my best friend. Kyle
By Kyle Danis

My mother is my hero because she gives me hugs and she loves me.
By Logan Lariviere

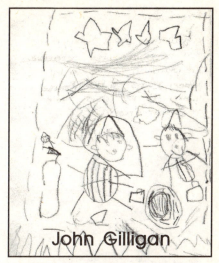

My cousin John Gilligan is my hero because he plays with me a lot when I go to his house when it's not cold. He's my best friend.
By Logan Watt

Mommy is my hero because she helps me.
By Maysin Beaucage-Couchie

My dad is picking me up real high at my house.
By Melissa Zaba

OUR HEROES IN PICTURES

My brother is my hero because he is nice and plays with me all the time.
by Miigwans Assance-Goulais

My Mommy and Dad are my heroes because they sometimes bring me to the store and buy me a toy or a treat.
By Owen Smart

My brother is my hero because he hugs me.
By Ravin McLeod

Spiderman is my hero because I love him.
By Riley Ferrigan

OUR HEROES IN PICTURES

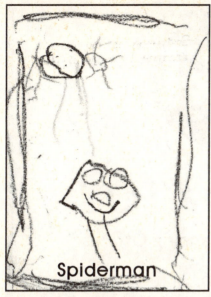

Spiderman

Spiderman is my hero because he saves the day.
By Riley Lavergne

Daphne

Daphne is my hero because she helps take care of me.
By Tia Solomon

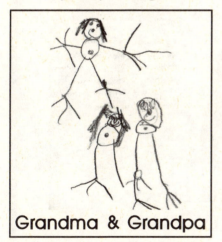

Grandma & Grandpa

My grandpa is my hero because he gives me rides down the stairs. My grandma is my hero because she saved my brother Marcus from the deep water.
By Shandace Couchie

Jesse Menard

I, Jesse, am my hero because I save people from big fish.
By Jesse Menard

GRAND&TOY®
Performance Enhancing Offices™

Since 1882, Grand & Toy has been the one trusted source that Canadian businesses have turned to for all of their office supplies and money-saving solutions.

**480 Cassells Street
North Bay, ON P1B 8J5
(705) 476-1000**

Monday - Friday: 8:00 AM - 6:00 PM
Saturday and Sunday: Closed

Be someone's hero and restore a bit of their past today!

Your children will cherish your old photos when our experts bring them back to life. Bring in any old photo for a no charge quote today and have them ready as a gift that they will have for all time. All this for as little as $39.95.

WARNING: restored

Photo Metro
foto source™

191 Lakeshore Drive
North Bay, Ontario
Phone: 705-472-9311

Or visit us at:
www.photometro.ca

Northgate Square
North Bay, Ontario
Phone: 705-476-2028

Add some **COLOUR** to your business!

Banners
Banner Stands
Brochures
Business Cards
Cheques
Flyers
Graphic Design
Invoices
Letterhead
Post Cards
Promotional Items
Rack Cards
Sandwich Boards
Signs
Trade Show Booths
T-shirts
Vehicle Decals

Choose Creative to make your Company stand out from the rest.

creative BUSINESS FORMS

SUSAN CALICIURI
creativebf@gmail.com

Toll Free: 1.866.301.1102
Local: 705.475.1211
Fax: 705.497.7525

Add some COLOUR to your business!

T 705.475.1211 / 1.866.301.1102
F 705.497.7525
E creativebf@gmail.com
W creativeforms.ca

LES ALIMENTS M&M MEAT SHOPS

NORTH BAY LOCATIONS

245 Lakeshore - 495-1833

180 Shirreff Ave. - 497-7920

North Bay Literacy Council

Whether you need help with reading, writing, spelling, math or computers, the North Bay Literacy Council is there to help!

www.northbayliteracycouncil.ca

Our thanks to the North Bay Literacy Council for all the wonderful work they do in the community . . . you're our **HERO!**

DENT'S CAMERA CENTRE

168 Oak St. W
North Bay, ON

705-475-0341

429 Main Street East, North Bay, ON P1B 1B6
705-497-1733

Soul Sister Creations

Soul Sister Creations offers a specialty shopping experience that celebrates woman and her diversity through the sale of unique items made by Canadian woman-makers. Our doors are open to all women and the people who love them.

A-170 Oak Street West, North Bay, ON P1B 2S7
705-478-9473

CREATIVE LEARNING

Your Neighbourhood Toy Store

www.creativelearning.ca

181 Main Street West, North Bay, Ontario P1B 2T6
(705) 472-9832

Harmony House

- *Relieve Stress* • *Energize*
- *Re-Focus* • *Reiki Master*

Suzanne Harmony
1531 CASSELLS STREET
NORTH BAY, ON 705-472-9005

WATCH FOR OUR NEW BOOK SPRING 2009

Leap of Faith, from Fear to Fulfillment
By Suzanne Harmony

CHAPTER TEN

OUR CELEBRATED HEROES

Fame is not the glory, virtue is the goal, and fame only a messenger to bring more to the fold.

Vanna Bonta

Al Gore

Spring 2007 is when Al Gore first inspired me. It was in class. We were watching his documentary, 'An Inconvenient Truth'. When he got to the part where he showed how much $CO2$ there was in our air and that in the next 50 years we would be in trouble, I was shocked. When he got to the part where we could help, I listened to every word. He talked about how if we recycle more, if we use energy-efficient appliances, if we use electric or fuel-efficient vehicles, if we don't waste water and if we turn off the lights when we're not using them, then this will help our planet.

From then on, I pledged to help save the planet a little at a time. I started by recycling anything I could to cut down on garbage. Next, I started to cut back on the amount of water I used. I started using less electricity in my daily life. I also started urging my parents to idle the car a little less.

Then, I really started to notice everything that everyone was doing to help the environment. My class planted a tree in the school yard. Everyone was recycling everything they could. I tried to help the planet a little at a time and it worked. Global warming effects us all, and we can stop it. Thank you, Mr. Gore for inspiring me to help save the planet!

By Anthony Caliciuri, age 11

Rosa Parks

Rosa Louise McCauley Parks, mieux connue sous le nom de Rosa Parks, est ma héroïne à cause d'un jour historique. C'est un jour que plusieurs personnes vont avoir dans leur mémoire. Elle va toujours être dans la mienne. Elle a fait quelque chose qui a choqué le monde entier.

En 1955, le premier décembre, Rosa Parks a refusé d'aller à l'arrière de l'autobus. Dans ce temps, les personnes de race noir ne pouvaient pas s'asseoir où ils voulaient dans l'autobus. Les personnes de race blanche, comme moi, avaient plus de droits et libertés dans l'autobus et dans la vie de tous les jours.

Elle est une héroïne pour moi parce que même si elle savait qu'elle pourrait aller en prison, elle a combattu pour la justice et ça c'est une vraie héroïne.

Par Ashley Rose Bénard-Legris, 10

Dale Earnhardt Jr.

Dale Earnhardt Junior is my hero because he doesn't cry when he loses the race.

By Jacob Rogers, 5

Terry Fox

Terry Fox is my hero. He had a terrible sickness. This sickness got into his leg so the doctors cut it off. He ran around with a flat foot for money. The terrible sickness got to his lungs and he died. The doctors use the money he got to help people with this sickness.

By Rory Macpherson, 6

Sarah McLaughlin

Sarah McLaughlin is not only a wonderful singer but also a wonderful role model to me. When I play hockey and need some encouragement, I think of her and sing her encouraging songs 'Black Bird' and 'Building a Mystery'.

She is also my hero because she supports animals. She has starred in commercials speaking out against animal cruelty. She was kind to put her song "Memory" in the background of the commercial. I've told many people I know about her and the important role she plays with animals. Sarah McLaughlin is one of a kind.

By Brooklyn Ladouceur, 10

Kyle Shewfelt

Kyle Shewfelt was the Olympic gold medalist for floor in 2004. Two years later, in 2006, I was having a tough time with gym. I wasn't having fun. I was being yelled at. I was having trouble being happy. I just got depressed whenever I walked in there. But then I saw Kyle on T.V. He was giving a speech about his inspiration. He said that he was starting to have trouble in gym. He said that when he was young, he decided he didn't like it anymore. But then, he thought, what if.

His answer was greatness. It's not just the ability to flip in the air a million times but to prove to yourself that anything is possible if you just try. Those words hit me. I was having the same problem so I tried it. And guess what? I'm still doing gym. Kyle helped me through my time and that was big for me. So from that day, my love for gymnastics came back. I said, "One day I'll show Kyle that truer words were never spoken".

By Taylor Jones, 12

Wayne Gretzky

Wayne Gretzky is my hero because he was a great hockey player. He played for the Edmonton Oilers, Los Angeles Kings, St. Louis Blues and the New York Rangers. He played from 1979 to 1999. He is from Brantford, Ontario. He is now part-owner and head coach of the Phoenix Coyotes. I chose him as my hero because I want to be like him when I'm older. Someday, I would like to meet him because he might tell me some tricks on how to play hockey like he did.

By Alex Arnott, 7

Sidney Crosby

My hero is Sidney Crosby. He's my hero because I want to be a hockey player like him when I grow up. He is twenty years old and his birthday is August 7th. The number on his jersey is 87. He plays for the Pittsburgh Penguins. He is my hero because I admire him. I always watch hockey games when he is playing. His team always wins.

By Ross Welch, 7

Lucky ⭐ 13

IS PROUD TO SALUTE
THE HERO IN ALL OF US!!!

McKeown Ave.

Callander

Lower Airport

Upper Airport

Sage Rd.

North Bay Home Solutions

Realty Ltd / Brokerage

www.northbayhomesolutions.com

409 McIntyre St. W., North Bay
705.475.2222

www.northbayhomesolutions.com

You've seen our signs, now meet our team!

Cleo Laframboise,
Broker

Daryle Kachan,
Sales Representative

Kelly Maxwell,
Sales Representative

Marc Girard,
Sales Representative

Matt Laframboise,
Sales Representative

Murray Powers,
Broker of Record

Robert Landry,
Sales Representative

Tammy Malcolm,
Sales Representative

Val Beaver,
Sales Representative

Renée LaVictoire,
Sales Representative

Cindy Bilz
Admin

**TEAM
TRUST
TRADITION**

Lynn Bedard
Admin

CHAPTER ELEVEN

OUR AUNTS AND UNCLES

When you look at your life, the greatest happinesses are family happinesses.
                                        Joyce Brothers

Trevor Alcock

My uncle is one of the most fun guys in the world. His name is Trevor. Whenever I'm sad or feeling down, he always has a funny joke to cheer me up. He can also be a big help. Once he, my parents and I were at the mall buying groceries. When we were at the register, he saw a stapler. He picked it up and said, "I'm going to staple your hat." I didn't know what he meant. I understood, "I'm going to staple your hand!" So I moved my hand over my head and I hit the stapler, putting a staple into my middle finger. He felt so bad. Everyone tried to find a way to get it out. Then, my uncle pulled out his pocket knife and pulled the staple out. We still talk about that, even though it happened when I was four!

We always have good times together. He takes me to the trailer. Sometimes, I watch movies with him and do all kinds of stuff that's fun. He also goes to a lot of places in Southern Ontario. He tells me a lot of things about some of the attractions so that if I go to a town, I know what to do. And if I do go, I have the best time.

Once, he took me to a town he told me about. We rented a red van and we told jokes all the way. But, he doesn't always travel. Sometimes, he stays at home and watches some movies and invites me over. He was the one who first showed me the movie, "Star Wars".

I usually ride my bike over or my parents eat supper there. We still have a lot of fun. He has a computer with lots of games. We play a whole bunch of games all night. I always win.

He also likes hockey, so we talk about how many wins and how many losses the teams have. We talk about suspensions and all that stuff. The time I spend with my uncle is some of the best times ever.

by Fraser Duhaime, 11

Marian Poirier

Auntie Marian has shown me that one person can make it through anything and keep going. She has the most strength and courage of anyone I know. She has made it through the loss of my dearest Uncle Coco (her husband) one January, only to lose my sweetest cousin Bryan (her son) only one year later. If I could only have her strength and courage, I believe I could make it through anything life has to offer. That is why my Auntie Marian is my hero.

By Shawnee Penasse, 10

Uncle Bert

My hero is my uncle, Bert. He was in the war fighting to make peace in the world. My uncle Bert is still alive. He got shot in the head. My uncle Bert taught me a lot of stuff like how to hunt and shoot a gun. My uncle Bert told me lots of stories about the war when I was a little boy and how hard it was to walk through strong and deep creeks.

By Brody Knight

Greg Grisé

Hi! I'm Cecilia. My uncle Gregory is in the military right now and I miss him. My uncle is very nice and he is a talented cook. He learned how to cook in Italy, Vancouver, Florida, Quebec and Toronto.

My uncle Gregory taught me how to cut a cucumber a different way. You hold it sideways, cut through the middle and then cut sideways until you have no room left. My uncle Greg is a great cook, but he takes time to teach me how to cook too. He joined the military and did basic training in Quebec. He tried his best to train hard and he didn't quit.

My uncle has many talents: cooking, drawing, inventing and teaching. Even though his talents are hard to do, he shares them with others. Now that he is in the military, he is using his talents to serve all Canadians!

By Cecilia Mogan, 9

John Campeau

Uncle Grease was like a dad to me. He was always there for me if I ever needed him. He was in the hospital when I was sick. He was there just to watch movies with me. Our favourite movies to watch were The Wizard Of Oz and Charlie's Angels. I miss him every day. He died on May 11, 2007 of liver cancer, which he had fought for three years. My uncle Grease was a very funny man. He made people laugh. He had many friends and a family that loved him every much. I was by his side when he went to the spirit world but I know he is still here with me, in my heart. I miss him so much . . .

By Bella McLeod, 11

Catherine Mathias-MacDonald

My hero is my Auntie Catherine because she is a role model for all people. She grew up on Bear Island, which is a small Ojibway community with a very small school. From a young age, she wanted to be a lawyer. She stayed in school and worked very hard. She is now a lawyer in North Bay.

My auntie and I like to hang around together. She is very good to me and helps my mom and dad by taking me when they are busy. We like taking the dogs to the park. One is named Jackson, another Milo, and my dog is Lola.

She takes me out for dinner and sometimes to the show. She also takes me to hockey. When she babysits Hannah, she lets me stay overnight to help her with the baby. I really like to take care of Hannah. Everyone should have a wonderful auntie like mine. I love you, Auntie "C".

By Amber Mathias, Grade 3/4

Kim Munro

My Auntie Kim showed courage for going to Afghanistan and being a part of the army. It takes a lot of courage to go to a place where there are bombings, shootings and people dying. She's my hero.

My aunt joined the Canadian Armed Forces when she was 17 years old. She started training in 1992. Her husband is also in the army. She was scared when her husband had to go because that's when Afghanistan started to get dangerous.

My aunt has gotten the CD medal and the General Campaign Star. The CD medal is for having completed 12 years of loyal service to the forces and the General Campaign Star is for her service in Afghanistan.

When she goes to Afghanistan, my Uncle Adam watches the children and when he goes, my Auntie Kim watches the children. Her children really miss her when she goes there but she gets them souvenirs. She sometimes misses their birthdays or Christmas. One time, I went with my cousins to a place where they had cameras set up for my aunt to speak to them and see her family.

I think she should get an award for courage because it takes courage to have a job where you could get injured.

By Kyesha Fong, 9

Jamie McQuaid

Where do I begin? Uncle Jamie was so amazing, words just can't describe. My uncle was the sweetest and most jubilant man I have ever met. He was the type of person who could brighten up a gloomy crowd just by entering the room. He was always so full of life. The thing that made him so wonderful was the fact that he never thought only about himself. He only thought about others. He sacrificed his time just to see someone smile. If he kept a list of all the good deeds he had done in his life, it could have wrapped around the world!

I spent as much time as I could with my uncle Jamie. I knew that he wouldn't be around forever. I treasured and cherished every moment with him. He always had on a smile on his face and could easily put a smile on yours.

When I was about 10, my parent's let me stay at my uncle's for two weeks, by myself, in Peterborough. When he and my aunt arrived at my house to pick me up, I knew that these two weeks would be something that I would remember forever. Within those weeks, we did many things together such as painting his boat, fishing, traveling, shopping, eating ice-cream, watching movies and more.

The thing that I remembered the most was one day, while we were driving, he saw a little boy fall off of his bike near the side of the road. When he saw this, he immediately stopped the car, got out and helped him up. He even fixed the bike. He could have simply gone on his way, acting nonchalant but instead, he decided to do a good deed. Sure, he was little late getting to his destination but that wouldn't have meant a thing to him. Seeing this act of kindness made me beam with happiness. There was clearly nothing this man wouldn't do to help someone.

About a year and half later, my uncle Jamie passed away from a heart-attack. Hearing this devastated me for a long time and a part of me was lost forever. This man was so close to me and then was taken away. I hate the fact that I'm never going to see him again but knowing all the good things he has done in his life inspires me to be like him. I know he made the world a little bit brighter. If only more people were like him, this world would be a much better place.

by Brittany Lauren Ashley Gale, 13

Derek Decaire

Derek 'the bolt' Decaire is my uncle and a constant reminder of why I do my best and why I am a good person on a daily basis. When I was a kid, I looked up, way up, to this man and felt stimulated and enthused by his very presence.

The tall, neatly-trimmed man is a kid at heart who, like my dad, never fails to amuse in every word that comes out of his mouth. He is a hardworking man who is never boring. He's vibrant. He and my father are like Abbott and Costello. They never tire out of a good show when they are together and I suppose that, to them, it is like old times on Alexander Road.

When I was small, my dad told me stories of the Bolt, on Alexander Road, and the adventures they were in together. Most of them were funny because of my wily and devilish uncle. There were fictitious stories of him being chased by police and having fun on their street, until it burned down.

He visits every now and then. I specifically remember a trip to Ottawa in which he brandished his new PSP with the excitement and pride that a kid might have with having the largest toy in his class. The way he acts is the result of living the great life he has. When I was told I had to write about someone who inspires me, someone who wants the absolute best for me, I'm glad I had such a great person to do it on.

By Greg Decaire, 13

Bryan Mullan

My hero is Uncle Bryan because he helps me do my math homework and teaches me about cars. He's funny all the time! Love you Uncle Bryan!

By Connor Mullan,

Cindy Belanger

Aunt Cindy doesn't have bionic bunny strength, nor is she a goddess among us but trust me, she has the sweetest heart. Last year, my grandpa Gerry was sent to the Sudbury hospital to have cancer treatment on his head. It was very hard for Cindy because he had been in a lot of pain and suffered every day. His weight had gone down and his mind had weakened. Aunt Cindy took care of him and helped the nurses fix the bandages. The pain was so much that the dressing had to be done fast and right.

Cindy also had to take care of her family and workload. My grandpa was sent back home to North Bay. Cindy would come every weekend and help take care of him in the hospital, knowing he would die in great pain. Months had gone by and he passed away. The journey was hard for everyone but he was finally at peace with his wife. Lung cancer had taken their mother's life 14 years ago.

A few weeks later, after everybody tried to move on with their lives, we received another phone call from Aunt Cindy that her house had burned down. The blue boxes that were outside caught on fire in the hot sun. It was so hard for my aunt because they had been redoing their house for three years and were almost finished. The difficult part was that all her memories were gone, like pictures of her mom and dad, birth certificates and her youngest son, Zach, also lost his hamster friend. Luckily, her whole family was out camping when this happened because her house burned down in four minutes and there would have been no survivors. My aunt Cindy always kept strong through the bad experiences and never lost faith. Even after having to move into her in-laws' house with her two sons and husband, she still kept strong.

The Belanger family is still not in their home but hopefully by May 2008, they can open the doors of their new home and start a new chapter in their lives. I no longer have to think of what a hero is. Now I finally know, Aunt Cindy.

By Alanah Maureen Côté, 12

Todd and Gwen Schofield

174 MAIN ST. E., NORTH BAY, ON
705.472.0110

DEBT CONSOLIDATION • MORTGAGES

A Better Place For You

**HOME
LIFE
INVESTMENTS
RSPs
FINANCIAL PLANNING
GROUP
DISABILITY
BUSINESS**

MICHAEL JOHNSON, CFP

MIKE JOHNSON INSURANCE SERVICES LTD.
326 Airport Road, North Bay ON P1B 8W9
Bus: 705-474-5900   Fax: 705-474-5995
Cell: 705-471-4222 Toll Free: 1-800-454-5902
After Hours Emergency Service: 1-800-465-2667

236 Worthington St. W., North Bay, ON P1B 3B4 (705) 476-7612

224 Airport Road, North Bay, ON P1B 8W6
guystiresales@cogeco.net (705) 495-0886

SPARE CHANGE

USED AND SURPLUS
OFFICE FURNITURE

755 Wallace Road
North Bay, ON, P1B 8G4
(705) 476-4000

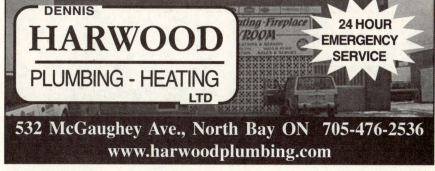

532 McGaughey Ave., North Bay ON 705-476-2536
www.harwoodplumbing.com

CHAPTER TWELVE

OUR FAMILIES

I don't care how poor a man is; if he has family, he's rich.
  Dan Wilcox and Thad Mumford,
  "Identity Crisis," M*A*S*H

Ivan & Rebecca Aubin
(Now and Forever)

My mommy and my daddy are my heroes because they are helping me get through my kidney problem. Even though they are not so thrilled about traveling to Ottawa and back to North Bay, they know it is to help me. They make sure that all my medications and all the things that need to be tended to are done. They give me a normal life and always make sure I am happy, even though I can tell they are sometimes sad. No matter how frustrating it can be they will not let me feel sad. They always tell me that it is ok and that I will be fine. They encourage me to follow my dreams. They give me their strength when I need it. In a few years, I will have to get a transplant. It costs $125,000.00. I am scared. I can't believe the price but no matter what, they are going to make sure that I get the transplant to save my life.

There are so many things that I can say as to why my mommy and my daddy are my heroes. I have many other people in my life that I love and are my heroes. My memere and pepere, my cousins Kyle and Jamie, my sister Kendale and a close friend of my mom's, named Jaime. Jaime did not even know me, but when she met my mom and knew that one day I would need a transplant, she said that she would give hers to me if it was a match. That takes a real special person to do something so important. All these people always come to the rescue and always act normal around me, even though I know they are scared about my kidney problem. I am so lucky to have so many heroes in my life. I feel so loved and they make me feel like a hero.

By Courtney Aubin, 11

Tyler Martin
(The Boy Who Touched many Hearts)

When choosing a hero, people select someone they know personally. For me, it's a little different. He is my older brother Tyler and even though I have never met him personally, I believe we have a connection and that one day I will find that connection.

Tyler was born December 29th, 1986. It almost feels like I was there the day he was born. It feels like I could see the sparkles in my mom's eyes when she held him for the first time. A year passed by and Tyler seemed like a normal, happy, energetic little boy until my parents started noticing a big change in his behaviour. About a month later, they were told that he was suffering from a rare lung disease. The one way to cure his sickness was to receive a double-lung transplant as soon as possible. Those tears of happiness soon turned to tears of sorrow.

Tyler succumbed to his illness on December 2, 1991 while waiting for his double lung transplant. He was just four years old. Tyler's charm for life made an impact not only on him but on everyone around him. Hearing the words, "Your son might not make it through Christmas," is heartbreaking and I can't imagine how it must have felt for my mom, dad and brother Ryan.

This little boy touched the hearts of North Bay as he was desperately fighting for his life. He was the focus of a city-wide fundraiser that raised $50,000 to help pay for the expenses while he was in Toronto, awaiting the lung transplant that didn't arrive in time.

About three years later, my mom gave birth to my brother Zack and myself. As we grew up, we didn't quite understand what had happened in the past. Eventually, as we got older, we started to understand what had happened and the impact he made on everyone's life. Tyler is not with us now but I know, deep down, that his spirit lives on forever and always will.

By Chelsea Lynn, 14

Madeleine & Loren Chadbourn

Mes grands parents sont des personnes spéciales qui sont allés au-delà des attentes pour pouvoir garder cinq enfants qui ont perdu leurs parents tragiquement.

Quand ma mère avait deux ans, ses parents ont été tués dans un accident d'auto à cause d'un conducteur qui était en état d'ivresse. Les actions impardonnables du conducteur a fait que cinq enfants ne pourront jamais revoir leurs parents. Le plus jeune avait 2 ans et le plus âgé avait 15 ans.

La mère de ma mère avait sept frères. Un des frères a demandé s'il pouvait adopter les cinq enfants pour pouvoir les garder ensemble sous un même toit. Il avait deux garçons et un encore dans le ventre de sa femme. Quand même, lui et sa femme les ont gardés et les ont soignés.

Je pense que mes grands-parents sont magnifiques et courageux et je les aime beaucoup.

Par Carter Hodgson, 10

Crystal Swackhamer

My older sister Crystal is someone very special to me. She is disabled and has autism but she helps me read. She reads really well. She helps me do a lot of other things too. She plays with me, outside, all of the time. I also try to help her do things. Even though she is disabled, she can still do many things that normal people can do. She is my best friend. She often helps me when I am afraid of things. She'll hug me and tell me that she loves me. It makes me feel real good and happy. She is the bravest person I know.

By Samantha Swackhamer, 8

Helga & Heinz Weiskopf

My oma and opa, Helga and Heinz Weiskopf, came from Germany and Africa. They are two individuals who are hard working, loving and extremely creative. I find that my grandparents are hard working people because, even though they are older, they still go outside to look after all the animals on their farm. My grandparents are always working one hundred percent in everything they do.

Oma works hard with her cooking and in her garden, which has won best garden several years in a row. When Opa starts a project, he gives it his best and doesn't quit until he is sure things are done right. For example, when he does a draft on the computer, it's difficult for my oma to get him to stop.

They are also the most loving people I have ever met. Every day after school, since they are my neighbours, I will go over to their house and my oma will give me one of her famous oma hugs and will give me a piece of her homemade German tortes, cookies or fruit. Opa, on the other hand, is the kind of guy that says hello, gives you a hug and asks you about your day. Then he starts telling those stories of his, about different subjects that are just funny with the way he puts things.

The reason I had mentioned that they are so creative is because they are the reason I like art so much. As some people would put it, they are my inspiration. Because my opa is a well-known contractor from this area, everytime I have a

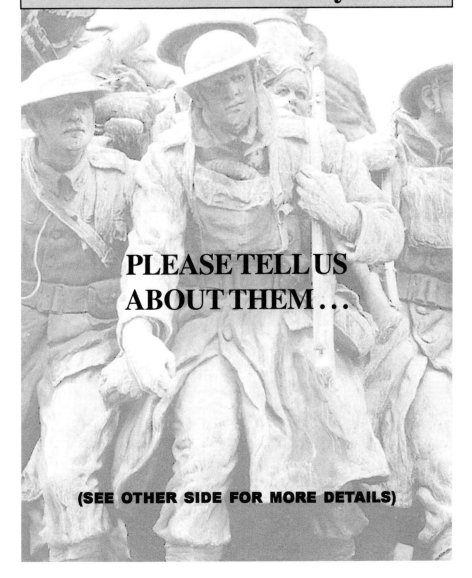

Please go to: **MyHeroTroops.com**
Click on: **Submit a story for the first time**
Click on: **CANADIAN TROOPS**
And input your story.

Both of your names will appear in our new book!

project that involves building something, he tries to help out. The cool thing is that he always comes up with intriguing little ideas that improve the projects.

My oma is also a strong influence in the creative part of my life. Every holiday, she is the one who decorates the entire house all by herself with her handmade crafts or collections. In spring, it's her frog collection and in winter, she brings out her Santas. So she is pretty easy to buy for. My oma and opa are just the kind of people that lighten up your day with their warm hugs and great personalities.

Joshua MacDonald, 12

Marketa

About two years ago, I went to visit my relatives in the Czech Republic. When we arrived in Prague, my cousin had come to pick us up. He's about 30. He drove us all the way from Prague to another big city called Brno (Ber-no). That's his home town. When we arrived at his house, we were greeted by his wife and his three daughters. We ate lunch and then one of his daughters, Barbora, showed me the computer and we played Zoo Tycoon in Czech. It was fun!

The next day, I got up last because of the time change. We had breakfast and my dad said that we were going to my other cousin's house. There, we were greeted by my cousin's daughter, Marketa. She was one year younger than myself and she spoke really good Czech. We went upstairs and we went on the computer. We played a game called "Rex". It was really fun. My cousin's daughter, Barbora, was there too and she kept on getting angry at me because I was calling her Brambora, which means "potato" in Czech. Marketa taught me a lot of Czech and I taught her English, too.

The next day, Marketa asked me if I wanted to go to school with her and I agreed. "If my mom is your cousin, then you must be my aunt," she exclaimed. So, I quickly started giving her orders! Once we got to school, everybody was looking at me because they knew I was the girl from Canada. I was so embarrassed. We got to the classroom, the teacher greeted us with a bunch of questions about Canada. While they were doing school work, I drew a picture. Finally, it was time for art. We crafted some clay and I made a flower. School was over and I had made a bunch of new friends. I still remember Marketa to this day and I still have her art project.

By Michelle Babak, 12

Brooklyn Thompson

My cousin, Brooklyn, is five years old and disabled. Both her arms and leg joints don't bend. When I found out she was disabled, I was very sad. She goes to the same school as me. She is in the JK/SK classroom. She has lots of friends and the part that makes her my hero is that she still walks and tries to fit in the best that she can.

By Brent Commanda, 9

Andrea Cousineau

My hero is my cousin because she carries me when I fall off my bike. I love her because she picks red roses.

By Sabrina Barrett, 5

Shaelyn Laronde

My hero is my sister Shaelyn. She is diabetic and she thinks that she has it rough, but she doesn't. She also has some good times. The reason that she has good times is because of her diabetes. For example, really soon, she is going to be interviewed by the Diabetic Research Foundation and I think this is really cool but she thinks it is kind of scary. I think the reason that she thinks it is scary is because she has to always be careful of what she eats. If she eats too much or too little, then she could get really sick.

If her sugar is high, then she can get real grumpy. If her sugar is low, then she can get a headache and she can become real grumpy. She is also my hero because she is my little sister and she makes my life special. She can sometimes get on my nerves but that is her job as my little sister.

By Vanessa Laronde, 10

Carolyn & Ron Clark

Grandma and Grandpa are my heroes because they would never hurt me. When I was a baby, Grandma was the kindest person I ever met. She is my favourite person in my family. She is the greatest and she is beautiful. She is great, so great! I never want her to die. My grandma and grandpa are my heroes because they make me happy and they make me feel better when I feel sad. I love Grandma and Grandpa. Thank you for all of your hard work. You are the best grandparents! I love you.

By Mackenzie Clark, 6

Serena Foisy & Katie Hokstad

My uncle Mike has a Sugar Shack in Bonfield where he makes and sells maple syrup. My cousin, Serena, and my sister, Katie, and I were visiting his shack one day and we decided to go for a walk in the woods. On our walk, we put some clean snow in a bucket to roll the maple toffee in when we got back. We were all stuffed to our limits from eating tons of maple candy and maple sugar. We decided that we had gone too far into the woods, so we decided to turn back. Before we started to turn back, we decided to take a rest under a tree because we were all tired. We talked of how stuffed we were from maple candy and maple sugar, and how we might be too stuffed for maple toffee.

We finally decided that we were rested enough and we got back up to continue our hike. We stretched so that we did not get cramps. We continued the opposite way we came. At one point, the path did not look the same. We then realized that we did not take the same route. I thought I saw another path but when I stepped on it, I realized that it was snow-covered ice. I broke through. I could feel a strong current against my legs but there was ice around me so I could not be swept under. The current was too strong for me to lift myself out. Katie and Serena realized what was happening and came running over, managing to jump the creek. Katie stayed and tried to pull me out of the water while Serena tried to find her way back to get help. My sister finally pulled me out and Serena came back with help. I am grateful to them for saving my life.

By Hans Hokstad, Age 10

Lark & Les Bonnah

My heroes are my mom and dad, Lark and Les, because they love me. They help with my homework and they help me get ready for school. I am a lucky girl!

By Miyah Bonnah, 6

We build strong kids,
strong families,
strong communities

Plus de vie à la vie
des jeunes, des familles
et de la communautè

YMCA

YMCA Early Learning Children's Serivces

Providing high-quality educational child care for more than 150 years - Infancy to 12 Years

YMCA, Chippewa Early Learning Children's Centre (Infancy to 12 years)
186 Chippewa Street West, North Bay, ON - 497.1915 Ext. 227 or 237

YMCA, E.W. Norman Early Learning Centre (3.8 to 12 years)
599 Lake Heights Road, North Bay, ON - 476.2480

YMCA, Gertrude Early Learning Children's Centre (18 months to 12 years)
73 Gertrude Street, North Bay, ON - 476.7590

YMCA, St. Francis School-Age Program (3.8 to 12 years)
68 Gertrude Street, North Bay, ON - 476.7590

YMCA, St. Theresa Early Learning Children's Centre (18 months to 12 years)
1475 Main Street North, Callander, ON - 752.3277

YMCA, École publique Héritage Early Learning Centre (18 months to 12 years)
2345 Connaught, North Bay, ON - 472-8282

YMCA Early Learning Home Child Care Services (Infancy to 12 years)
186 Chippewa Street West, North Bay, ON - 497.1915 Ext. 244 or 236

www.ymcanorthbay.com

A financial security plan for all stages of life

It's never too early or late to plan for your financial security. Together, we can build a financial security plan that fits your needs as your life changes, and helps you achieve your financial security goals.

Freedom 55 Financial offers London Life's own brand of savings and investments, retirement income, life insurance, and mortgages, and financial products from other financial institutions. A London Life subsidiary, Quadrus Investment Services Ltd., offers exclusive mutual funds through Quadrus Group of Funds.

Please contact us today for more information.

Freedom 55 Financial in North Bay
1350 Fisher Street, 2nd Floor
705-472-7790
www.freedom55financial.com

Freedom 55 Financial   **QUADRUS**
Quadrus Investment Services Ltd.

Freedom 55 Financial is a division of London Life Insurance Company.

Freedom 55 Financial and design are trademarks of London Life Insurance Company. Quadrus Investment Services Ltd. and design are trademarks of Quadrus Investment Services Ltd. used with permission by London Life Insurance Company.

North Bay's Leading Full-Service Resort & Convention Centre

Clarion Resort
Pinewood Park

A fresh sense of business & relaxation.

For reservations call 705-472-0810
201 Pinewood Park Dr., North Bay ON P1B 8Z4
Tel: (705) 472-0810 / 1-800-461-9592 Fax: (705) 472-4427

stay@ClarionResortPinewoodPark.com
www.ClarionResortPinewoodPark.com

Hwy 11/17
1525 Seymour Street,
North Bay, ON
P1B 8G4
(705) 495-1133

THANK YOU
TO OUR
HOCKEY HEROES
FROM YOUR
FANS IN
NORTH BAY
AND AREA!

419 Haig Street (corner of Fisher St), North Bay
705-474-1850

www.northbaydaycare.com

De-Clutter Coach
Moreen Torpy, Professional Organizer
I will simplify the complex for you
705-476-0708
http://www.decluttercoach.ca/   info@decluttercoach.ca

TROUT LAKE TRADING COMPANY
3761 TROUT LAKE RD.   497-3508

The Plan
by **IG Investors Group**™

Investors Group Financial Services Inc.

Bob Ramsey	Susie Reid
Mark Entwistle	Kevin Reid
Hal Kenty	Todd Shillington
Roger Maille	Jason Taillefer
Ray Smith	Kathy Hurst
Lorne Byers	Jason Stapley
Michel LeBoeuf	Sarah Smith
Kevin Wilton	Abby Frangione
Susan Weiskopf	Dan Ransom
Tracy Govier	Mike Morin
Jean Chaput	Jason Ricci
Robb King	Niamh O'Shea
Maria Cadorette	Jaime-Lynn Chaulk
Ken Hastie	Steven Simpson
	Will Ouellette

1350 Fisher Street, North Bay, ON
705-472-4731

CHAPTER THIRTEEN

OUR PETS

If a dog jumps in your lap, it is because he is fond of you; but if a cat does the same thing, it is because your lap is warmer.

Alfred North Whitehead

Winston White

My dog, Winston, is a black lab and he's been there for me for most of my life. Winston was the outcast of his litter. He was the hyper one, just running around when all the rest of the puppies were sleeping or just trying to run. I was two and I really wanted a dog because I just got a new stepdad and having a new family isn't always easy, you know? Having my first word be 'doggy', I needed a dog. When we got there to pick out a puppy, it was really boring because the people were talking to my parents about things I didn't really care about. I just wanted to pick out a puppy and go home. That's when it hit me. No, I mean something really hit me and it had a slimy tongue too. I guess in this case, it's not the owner who picked the dog, but it's the dog that picked the owner.

So that's how it all started. Winston's a lot older now.; he's nine years old. There are so many stories going through my head that I can't even pick one. Okay, okay . . . I've got one. We got a Kong toy for Winston and we filled it with peanut butter. It was so funny to watch his tongue go up and down, from side-to-side for about 20 minutes until the peanut butter was gone. The Kong toy always felt and smelt like dog drool. We lost that toy one day and we have never found it again.

I love Winston and I wouldn't trade him in for anything, not for a turtle, a monkey or even a tiger. Winston's my hero so he isn't going anywhere except by my side for the rest of his life because he is certainly a friend forever.

By Victoria White, 12

Brutes Gaboury

I was combing my lovely hair when, all of a sudden, a fire-breathing dragon appeared and it took me away to his black cave in the forest. I was terrified. I screamed for help two times and a dog named Brutes the knight came. "Help me!" I cried. "Wuff, wuff!" he said. He got me down before the fire-breathing dragon came down and ate me.

The End

My dog Brutes is my hero because he saved me from getting hurt. I was playing in my yard and I slipped under the swing and he pulled me out.

By Avery Gaboury, 8

Nimosh Beaucage

Nimosh is a dog. When I go swimming, he thinks he is a lifeguard. When I go under water, he starts to bark, dives into the lake and swims to me. I grab onto his collar and he will drag me to shore.

Nimosh is just like a guard. When there is someone trying to sneak around, he starts to bark and goes wild. He is good for a two-year-old dog. He is also good at hunting. He helped my dad catch two moose by going into the bush and scaring them out. Nimosh is a good lifeguard, guard and hunter.

By Blake Beaucage, 7

Remington Murphy

Mon héros vient de Thunder Bay. Il a 13 ans et il est aussi mon animal. Il est mon chien et il s'appelle Remington. Mon histoire va t'expliquer pourquoi et comment il est mon héros. Ça va commencer avec une histoire triste...

Une jour d'été, Remington et moi étions dehors afin de pouvoir jouer dans l'arrosoir. Maman a remarqué une bosse qui se trouvait sur sa jambe gauche en arrière. On a décidé qu'après une semaine ou deux, qu'on allait va l'apporter au vétérinaire. La vétérinaire nous a dit qu'elle a trouvé un tumeur. Le tumeur n'était pas cancéreuse. On était très heureux d'entendre cette nouvelle. Elle a suggéré qu'on devrait enlever le tumeur. On a dit que c'était la meilleure chose à faire.

Cependant, après l'opération, nous avons eu peur. Lorsque nous sommes revenus du magasin, on est allé lui chercher et son pied était la grosseur d'une orange et il était très froid. Tout de suite, maman a téléphoné le vétérinaire pour lui dire que son pied est aggrandi. La vétérinaire a massé son pied et il est retourné à sa grandeur normale. Elle a trouvé que pendant l'opération, son équipe a probablement touché un de ses nerfs, qui a causé l'agrandissement.

L'opération du tumeur est correcte maintenant et on n'avait pas besoin d'amputer sa jambe. Il est mon héros à cause qu'il a survécu tout cela. Il est brave et est mon meilleur ami.

Par Taylor Murphy, 11

Hershey Newman

Hershey, my dog, is a black, grey and brown Shipoo. She is part Shitzu and part Poodle. We got her when she was seven weeks old and now she is two years old.

Hershey always protects me. One day, when we were walking in the bush and going down a hill, I suddenly fell and my leg was stuck in a hole, under a log. Hershey ran back up the hill to where I was and waited until I got my leg out.

Another reason she is special is that she got run over by a car and didn't die or break any bones. We were so happy that she was okay!

By Avery Newman, 8

Trooper the Dog

One boring, hot, summer evening after supper, I was sitting on the porch of my step-grandma's cottage. Her cottage is on a very small lake in Quebec. I saw her coming out of the bush but I didn't want to talk with her.

She said, "What are you doing?"

"I'm bored," I sighed. But then I realized that I shouldn't have said that because she was going to give me the lecture about when she was a kid and she was never bored. So I thought fast and said, "I'm going for a walk." So I took my dog and just as I was about to leave, she told me to go to her sister's cottage across the lake and that she would meet me there.

When I got on the dirt road, it was six o'clock. I started to make my way up the road with Trooper running in front of me. I visited other cottages on the way (but only the people I knew). By the time I got to my step-grandmother's sister's place, it was 7 o'clock. I decided to go back after thirty minutes because it was getting dark and my step-grandma hadn't arrived yet. Ten minutes later, I arrived at a garbage disposal place.

There were three ways I could go; the way I had just come from, the way back to my step-grandma's and the way back to North Bay. Not knowing, I took the road back to North Bay. After twenty minutes, it started to storm. I decided that I must have taken a wrong turn at the garbage place.

When I got back to the garbage place, I took the turn that led to my step-grandma's sister's place. I kept going and I accidentally went on another road!

I followed my dog Trooper, trusting him with all my heart, as he sniffed our way home and, thanks to him, I got home safely.

By Tyler Breadmore, 12

Rino the Dog

My dog is super cool! He likes to play all day. He likes to help me with the laundry. He's always number 1. He is the best. He waits at the door for me when I come home. This is why my dog is a hero.

By Michael-Anthony Power, 8

CHAPTER FOURTEEN

HERO HIGHLIGHTS

Aspire rather to be a hero than merely appear one.

Baltasar Gracian

Mike Chayer

Daddy is my hero because when the chair falls over in the kitchen table he saves me and picks me up and picks up the chair too. When I have a cough, Daddy puts the medicine in my mouth.

By Matthew Chayer

Maidie Vossen

My sister Maidie likes to play with me and she loves to play dress up. It was just three years ago when it all happened. In 2005 Maidie Rose was a new traveler in the world.

I never stopped praying for my sister to be a girl. I finally got what I wanted! I love my sister and she loves me.

By Jessie Vossen

My Uncle Brent Summers

Uncle Brent taught me how to read. Do you know how he taught me how to read?

First, with comics, then with big comics and then chapter books. I am now reading Charlotte's Web, Stuart Little and the Trumpet of the Swan, all in one book.

By Cedric Summers

Brenda Ducharme

My mom is my hero because she checks on me and helps me with my work. She brings me to the hospital when I am hurt. I love her and she loves me too.

By Jerrod Ducharme

Vandi Kennedy

Mon héros est ma maman parceque ma mère m'aide à faire mon travail à la maison et elle fait mon souper.

By Tagen Giroux

Philip Guenette

My brother, Philip, is my hero. When we play basketball, he catches the ball so it doesn't hit me.

By Gracie Guenette

Andrea Parks

Mon héros est ma maman parce qu'elle marche pour le cancer. Elle aime les grands-mamans et les grands-papas. J'aime mon héros parce que c'est ma maman aussi. Elle aime aussi ce beau monde. Elle aime aller en auto pour regarder les grandes personnes et il y a beaucoup de personnes.

By Jacqueline Domander

Gail Beaucage-Commanda

My mom is my hero because she protects me. She doesn't leave me alone, she takes me for rides in a van and truck.

I know my mom loves me because she gives me lots of kisses. I like that because it makes me feel nice in my heart.

Syler Beaucage

Kevin Ferrigan

Dad brings me ice fishing and he brings me hunting and he makes me laugh. He is the best dad in the world.

Coleman James Ferrigan

Sandra Lawrence

My mom Sandra protects me when my brother is going to hurt me. She will send him away and it is usually to his room.

I love my mom very much because she does a lot for my brother and I and she loves hugs but not the tight ones.

By Katlin Watson

My Special Dad

My Dad is my hero because he didn't let the snake see me at my papa's trailer and I didn't want the snake to bite me.

By Jerrett Bakker-Orr

Stanley Kulikowski

My hero is my grandpa but at home I call him dad. My grandpa has taken care of me since I was one year old. He has very strong muscles. He is a good fisherman and brave. He is brave because he sits and waits a long time for a bear to come and knock over the trap.

By Michael Kulikowski

My Grandma

My grandma is my hero. When I fall off the swing or the slide, she catches me. She reads me a story when I go to visit her at Christmas.

By Ethan Trecartin

Rob Derosier

Mon héros est mon papa parce qu'il m'aide avec mon travail et j'aide mon papa à nettoyer son camion.

By Evan Derosier

Shawna Ollivier

My sister Shawna is my guardian angel. My sister loves me and I want to be just like her. I love my sister very much and she is the only sister I have.

By Hailey Ollivier

CHAPTER FIFTEEN

OUR FAITH HERO

Yes I am with you always, until the very end of time.

Jesus Christ

Jesus Christ

Jesus is my hero because He died for us. Jesus is my hero because He saved the earth! I do not know this but I think that Jesus has brown hair. I also love Him very, very much. Jesus even saved humanity from sin!

Jesus was our teacher. He came here to teach us how to forgive each other and to love yourself and other people. He also told us about God the Father. God loves us very much too; same with Jesus. Jesus told us about God the Holy Spirit, who is part of the blessed trinity and it is He who helps us follow truth, which is what Jesus taught us while He was on Earth.

I try my best to be just like Jesus but sometimes it doesn't go how I planned it. That's the part I hate. It bothers me a lot. When those plans go wrong it takes me one step away from being like Jesus. I really want to be like Jesus. I will give you a number of how much I want to be like Jesus -9999. That is how much I want to be like Jesus. Is that a big number or what? Some people have heroes that are pretend, (e.g. Spiderman), but my hero, Jesus, is real and I know I will get to see Him one day.

By Tony Fournier, 7

THANK YOU FOR READING OUR BOOK

We sincerely hope you enjoyed the stories and pictures.

Our team has worked very hard to make this
an inspiring and fun book for you.

We have done our best to ensure that all the
storywriter's names and all the heroes names have been
listed in the book.

IF...we have missed your name or story...
We are 100%...

SORRY

Please let us know so we can ask
for your forgiveness!!

Many blessings to you – the YOU'RE MY HERO team.

WE HAVE A GIFT FOR YOU...

Our sponsors have given generously to this cause so that we could donate $8.00 of every book sold to local charities.

The next section of the book is dedicated to our sponsors. As a THANK YOU to the sponsors, please take a moment to read through their ads. Next time you are out and about in the community, take a moment to stop by their place of business and say,

"I saw your ad in the You're My Hero™ book - Thanks!"

HERE IS OUR GIFT OFFER TO YOU.

Simply take a few minutes to answer the questions in the
SPONSOR QUIZ
(see next page)

E-mail your answers to: quiz@ymhbooks.com

We will send you a FREE e-copy of an interview that Barry Spilchuk did with Jack Canfield of Chicken Soup for the Soul®.

Jack discusses - Sudden Wealth - How to create an in-flow of money and how to manage and protect it.

SPONSOR QUIZ

E-mail us the answers to these 12 questions and we will send you a **FREE** e-copy of an interview that Barry Spilchuk did with Jack Canfield- the founder of Chicken Soup for the Soul® entitled SUDDEN WEALTH SYNDROME.

E-mail your answers to: quiz@ymhbooks.com

1) What is IVAN's restaurant offering for FREE?
2) How many ARCHITECT firms are listed in the OUR DADS chapter?
3) What are the four first names in the NO FRILLS ad?
4) What is on the tear-out card that Greco's placed in this book?
5) What is the name of the carpet/flooring store in the Seymour Plaza?
6) How many years has PJ Walsh, Master Jeweller, been in business?
7) What are the names of the FIVE local Hotel Sponsors?
8) What are the names of the three SPORTING goods stores?
9) Guy's Tire and Harwood Plumbing both offer 24-Hour Service for different things. What are the 24-hour services they are offering?
10) What is the YMCA's Web Address?
11) What is the name of the Trophy company listed in the OUR FRIENDS chapter?
12) How many drivers are pictured in the U-Need-A-Cab ad?

SUMMARY OF DONATIONS
for the first YOU'RE MY HERO BOOK

Nipissing Women's Transition House	$17,000.00
Fundraising - Minor Sports - Penny Tremblay	5,600.00
Chippewa Secondary School	1,200.00
W. J. Fricker Senior Public School	550.00
Nipissing Women's Transition House (EFAP)	500.00
West Ferris Secondary School	460.00
Vincent Massey Public School	440.00
Gathering Place Soup Kitchen (Kendall – Sinclair)	440.00
Rotary for Kids (Dan and Jamie EZ ROCK)	250.00
North Bay Food Bank (Cementation staff)	220.00
Near North Palliative Care (Tim Salidas)	200.00
Widdifield Secondary School	125.00
Habitat for Humanity (Mayor Vic Fedeli)	100.00
TOTAL as of October 2008	**$27,085.00**

SUMMARY OF BOOKS GIVEN TO CHARITY

Canadian Troops	1,600
Santa Claus Fund	750
Celebrate Marriage	100
Fundraisers	100+
Bonfield Library	48
Total	**2598**

DIARY OF A DREAM
The You're My Hero™ Story

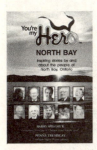

How does something like You're My Hero™ happen?

We were working on another dream - raising $100 million for charity, doing a cross-country golf tour. We had a 38-foot motor home and were cruising through our ninth state in the USA when gas prices hit an all-time high. It was costing us over $400.00 a day to fill up the bus.

I kept praying for two things: 1) A major sponsor to underwrite our travel costs 2) Something we could leave behind as a legacy in every city we visited across the USA and Canada.

Three different times, I received the same answer to my first prayer: "You are supposed to be your own sponsor." I felt like Bill Cosby when he did the God and Noah's Ark comedy routine many years back. Each time, I got the same answer to my prayer, "You are supposed to be your own sponsor," I would curiously reply, "Say what? We do not have enough money to fill the bus with gas for 30 days and You want me to sponsor myself for a year?!?"

A short while later, an answer to my second prayer came in the form of grade six, twin girls in Flint, Michigan. They asked a friend of mine, "Can we do a Chicken Soup-like book for our classroom?"

This dream has gone through many phases and stages since the fall of 2005. What has evolved is this system - the You're My Hero™ System. The system that ensures everyone is involved - no one is left out - non-profit groups benefit and people take the opportunity to acknowledge their friends, their family and sometimes even themselves.

As of October 1, 2008, we have our third book in progress and have fielded inquiries from numerous cities across Canada and the United States about doing You're My Hero™ books for their cities.

The golf dream will continue, in a few years, with a sponsor - You're My Hero™ Books Ltd. God was right again. He always is.

Thank you to everyone who has caught and are catching the Hero-Bug. The grade six twins asked the perfect question. Thanks girls!

To quote another good book, "…and a child shall lead them."

Barry Spilchuk

Do you know a women who has touched your life?

PLEASE TELL US ABOUT HER!

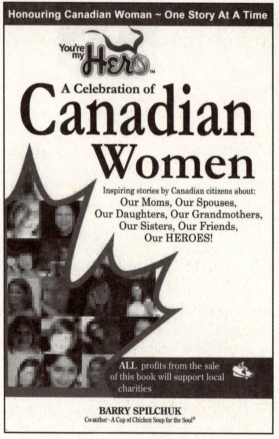

Please go to: **YMHbooks.com**
Click on: **Submit a story for the first time**
Click on: **CANADIAN WOMEN**
And input your story.

Both of your names will appear in our new book!

Do you know anyone who has served in the Canadian Military?

PLEASE TELL US ABOUT THEM

Please go to: **MyHeroTroops.com**
Click on: **Submit a story for the first time**
Click on: **CANADIAN TROOPS**
And input your story.

Both of your names will appear in our new book!

North Bay and District Chamber of Commerce

On behalf of the business community, Barry and Gerald would like the thank the Chamber of Commerce for over 100 years of **HEROIC SERVICE!**

A big THANK YOU to the media of North Bay and area for their support and enthusiasm.

Who Do You Know...
That would like to honour their heroes And raise money for charity in the process?

Here are just a few groups that can be served by:
YOU'RE MY HERO™ BOOKS

CITY

You're My Hero™ - CITY Books
Celebrate your local heroes just like the people of North Bay, Ontario. They raised money for Nipissing Transition House, a women's shelter. Money was also raised for school projects.

School Children

You're My Hero™ - SCHOOL Books
Every child in every grade can go home and say, "Mom and Dad, I'm going to be in a book with a Chicken Soup guy!" Enhance literacy in a simple way - each child has to write only ONE story and put it on-line. You also raise money for school projects!

Church Members

You're My Hero™ - CHURCH Books
The congregation is usually buying books in the Church bookstore, some of the books written by their Pastor. Why not let them WRITE the book about Heroes in your Church. You enhance the spirit of fellowship and raise a few dollars too!

Your Company Staff

You're My Hero™ - COMPANY Books
Acknowledging each other is the BEST way to grow your team and your company. For one flat fee let our team assemble a book about your team. It can enhance morale, teamwork and your bottom line!

Visit our website: www.YMHbooks.com
Call: 1-647-350-2327 / Email: barry.s@ymhbooks.com

To all the local *Heroes*

In special recognition of our Catholic District School Board for this excellent literacy initiative, and all the children who have contributed, keep up the great spirit of every day praise.

Our own children are a part of this book, and we are truly honoured.

- David Neil, President

24 x 7 On-Site
Computer Service

Bell World,
Century Centre Plaza

1-888-GET-NEIL

PENNY TREMBLAY

Penny Tremblay, ACG, CL
President
Northern Lights Presentations
www.PennyTremblay.com
705-498-1818

Penny will teach you concepts of:

- Effective Communication
- Relationship Strategies
- Work / Life Balance
- Time Management
- Team Building
- Leadership Development
- Effective Presentation Building and Delivery

If you are interested in writing to Penny Tremblay, receiving her free newsletter, *Leadership Tips*, or would like to inquire about speaking engagements, seminars or invite her to speak at an event, please direct all correspondence to:

Northern Lights Presentations
180 Sheriff Avenue, Suite 230
North Bay, Ontario Canada P1B 7K9
705-472-2528 ext. 202
info@northernlightspresentations.com
www.northernlightspresentations.com

The Right Decision Starts with Your People!

LIFE'S BRIGHTER
under the sun

Gerald Amond
Teresa O'Kane-Amond
705-752-2444
www.sunlife.ca

© Sun Life Assurance Company of Canada, 2008.

MEET YOUR CO-AUTHORS
GERALD G. AMOND

Gerald Amond was born Aug 10, 1959. Raised and educated in North Bay, he is a product of the Separate School System.

One of his first jobs was during high school when he worked as a part time custodian for the board.

He graduated from Canadore College, Marketing, in 1980 and accepted a position with Canada Packers in Toronto.

He married Teresa O'Kane in October 1980 and they recently celebrated their 28th anniversary.

Their son Matthew was born in 1982

They moved back to North Bay in 1987. Gerry left a successful career with Canada Packers so that they could raise their son in the same type of environment that he had enjoyed as a child.

He spent a short but fruitful time with an international Management Consulting firm as a sales manager before joining Mutual Life of Canada in the fall of 1989.

It was there that Gerry found his calling. The opportunity to assist families with their planning needs enabled him to enjoy the two things he loved most in business ~ Relationships and Sales.

The people that he has assisted over the past 20 years have become so much more than clients to him. He truly cares about each and every person he has come to know and it shows in the service that he provides.

Gerry has been active over the years with the Knights of Columbus where he is a Fourth Degree Knight. He has also helped various charities including Minor Hockey and Big Sisters.

Through the years he has shown time and again that his heart is as big as his will to succeed.

MEET YOUR CO-AUTHORS
BARRY SPILCHUK

Birthday: November 10, 1957 - Hamilton, ON
North Bay-ite: 1967-1978 and 1986 - 2008
Favorite Books: The Bible, The You're My Hero™ Books, Things I Overheard While Talking To Myself by Alan Alda
Favorite Movies: Mr. Smith Goes to Washington, It's a Wonderful Life The American President, When Harry Met Sally, Mr. Holland's Opus, Mamma Mia
Favorite TV Shows: West Wing, Mary Tyler Moore, Law & Order, M.A.S.H., Cheers, Studio 60, Seinfeld, Friends.

Favorite Teachers (just a few of many): Dr. Carruthers: Miss Nichols, Mrs. Smith & Roy Osburg; Centennial - Shirley Tayler, W.J. Fricker: Rick Ferron; Chippewa High: Christine Cassidy, Bud McMartin, Eric Jarvi, Miss Hanson and Floyd MacMillan; Canadore College: Robin Smallwood, Dean McCubbin, Ken Cork, Rod Vincent, and Berny McGuaghey; From the School of Life: Mom, Dad, Tim, Karen, Jamie, Chrissy and Mike Spilchuk. God, Jesus Christ, Leland Val Vandewal, Jack Canfield, Mark Victor Hansen, Berny Dohrmann, Martin Rutte, Dr. Robert H. Schuller, Tim Piering, Lisa Nichols, Sharan Ro, Lydia Hale, Joel Roberts, Kristin Shepherd, David Stanley, Paul Barton, and people in general.

Pet Peeves: Unfairness, when someone takes advantage of someone else, bullies in school or business, lying and rudeness.

Special Moments: The birth of our three "chimps." Our 25th anniversary. Every time I have apologized to one of our children. Being the first Canadian to coauthor a Chicken Soup for the Soul® book. Teaching for 11 years at a high-level business retreat in Los Angeles. Being asked to walk in the Labour Day parade by the labour council when I was Chamber of Commerce President. Saying "YES" to this dream. The book launch of our first You're My Hero™ book.

www.YMHbooks.com
1-647-350-2327
barry.s@ymhbooks.com